Web sites that work

52 brilliant ideas
one good idea can change your life...

Web sites
that work

Secrets from winning web sites

Jon Smith

Copyright © The Infinite Ideas Company Limited, 2005

The right of Jon smith to be identified as the author of this book has been
asserted in accordance with the Copyright, Designs and Patents Act 1988

First published in 2005 by
The Infinite Ideas Company Limited
Belsyre Court
57 Woodstock Road
Oxford
OX2 6HJ
United Kingdom
www.infideas.com

CIP catalogue records for this book are available from the British Library and
the US Library of Congress.

ISBN 1-904902-18-9

Brand and product names are trademarks or registered trademarks of their
respective owners.

Designed and typeset by Baseline Arts Ltd, Oxford
Printed and bound by TJ International, Cornwall

Brilliant ideas

Brilliant features

Each chapter of this book is designed to provide you with an inspirational idea that you can read quickly and put into practice straight away.

Throughout you'll find four features that will help you to get right to the heart of the idea:

- *Try another idea* If this idea looks like a life-changer then there's no time to lose. *Try another idea* will point you straight to a related tip to expand and enhance the first.

- *Here's an idea for you* Give it a go – right here, right now – and get an idea of how well you're doing so far.

- *Defining ideas* Words of wisdom from masters and mistresses of the art, plus some interesting hangers-on.

- *How did it go?* If at first you do succeed try to hide your amazement. If, on the other hand, you don't this is where you'll find a Q and A that highlights common problems and how to get over them.

Introduction

It's probably cost you thousands already. You're one of the children of the boom and when everyone who was anyone was buying up domain names and building web sites, your elbows were to the fore. But it hasn't done quite as well as you thought it would, has it?

It's not as jazzy as it should have been, and to be honest, it's all looking a little tired and jaded. And it's a little early for retro to be cool. You're getting visitors but they're not converting to customers; or worse, you simply aren't getting enough visitors. Mmmm. Are web sites just a waste of time, money and effort, a cunning invention of company IT departments to ensure their career longevity?

No. Web sites can be incredibly effective. But, like everything, you have to use the tricks of the trade and improve your offering if it's underperforming. You'll need to adapt or redefine what you have already; let's face it – that red background, yellow lettering and daft logo you chose all those years ago really are a bit naff. *Web sites that work* will show you how to achieve everything you want from your web site, help kick your competition into touch and impress the girls…Well, maybe not the latter, but still not bad for thirteen quid!

The keys to a web site that works are simplicity and usability – easy. So why should you read on? Well, paradoxically, building a web site that is both simple and easy to use is difficult and fraught with problems. Not in terms of coding issues, but because we tend to believe that everyone thinks like we do. They don't.

So how can I show you how to overcome these difficulties and problems in a mere 52,000 words? Simple – by showing you how to address the target user directly, in an organised and logical way, and using the right language. In a word, usability – for the marketeer, project manager, developer and designer – explained in the minimum number of words that are needed to address the points, and no more.

So why are there no illustrations or page grabs showing web sites that do work? Well, unless you are the same company, selling exactly the same products to the same audience, someone else's design won't work for you. If you are targeting different users, your design will have to reflect that; and if your budget for web design is different, you can reflect that too (though big doesn't always mean best). Each of the 52 brilliant ideas contained in this book will matter to you, in different ways and to different degrees.

Everyone knows somebody who can create a web site – developers are ten a penny (allegedly); but will they be able to deliver what you want? It's no good asking a team of developers to re-energise your web site without giving them a brief. We all have our own ideas about how things should work and look (and how much they should cost) so, with the best will in the world, if you don't tell the developers what you want, you won't get it (not even if you spend a whole penny). Before embarking on any of the chapters contained in this book, see if you can answer these questions. Do you know what you want from your web site? How easy is it to change the existing appearance, layout and functionality of your site? Would it be easier and more time efficient just to start afresh? How scalable is your site if things do improve? Will you have the bandwidth to handle the extra traffic, or will your site fall over? Most importantly, does your site portray the image you want? Can users find you? Who are they? Is anybody out there? Why do you need a web site? *Web Sites that Work* assumes no technical knowledge – that's what developers are for – but it should empower you to talk to the developers about what you want and, more importantly, what you don't want.

So how do you use this book? Dip in and dip out, read it from start to finish – it really doesn't matter (now you've bought it!). The 52 brilliant ideas contained within are generally quick fixes that should result in immediate benefits to your site, if adopted. If your budget is modest, implementing just a handful of ideas will still improve your web site and help you realise your ambitions and those of your company. Employ all 52 and your visitors really will be throwing themselves down on the floor and proposing – no wait, I mean buying more of your products, reading your information and coming back to your site, again and again and again...

1

Knowing me, knowing you, a-ha

There must be a strong business case for investing resources into a web site. Only when you understand what you want your web site to achieve will you be able to truly design an effective web site.

Step back, take a deep breath and listen to your web site's inner calling: 'Why am I here?' it cries...Well, cat got your tongue?

You weren't the only one affected by the hysteria created during the late nineties regarding web technology and our cyber-future...Stock prices were going off the chart, we all bought as many domain names as we could – in the hope that another company would buy them from us – and we all created web sites, spending hundreds, thousands and sometimes hundreds of thousands in the great race to be online...Fortunes were made and companies collapsed – for about three years, we all went completely barmy.

Sadly, in the rush to get online and command a presence on the World Wide Web a lot of companies and individuals paid over the odds for a site that was either design heavy and completely ineffective or poorly designed and scared or offended its users. So here you are, a few years on, a little bit older and hopefully wiser, with the opportunity to lick your wounds and re-energise your web site.

Write down ten values that you think your web site encapsulates. Now go to your web site and find examples of how these values are represented. Easy to write the list, difficult to see it put into practice, isn't it? If you can find examples of all ten, ask a friend (not a colleague) to work from the list. If they can't find examples of all ten, your web site isn't doing its job properly. Remember, I don't think like you and you don't think like me. Take this to the macro level and it quickly becomes obvious that you must test your design on others to truly gauge its effectiveness.

RETURN TO SENDER

It's a well-bandied phrase, but it's time to go *back to basics*. Yes, it's time to round up your key personnel (or maybe just you and the cat), a flip chart and some sticky notes, and iron out the why, the how and the who you are? Web sites can portray a whole host of images and emotions in users' minds, so you have to be clear before you begin the design and implementation of a site that what you are planning to create is actually what you want. If you are selling products, is that made clear right from the outset? If you are an information provider, how can this information be accessed? Do you know who your target audience is and does your site reflect this?

THE WHY

'I need a web site, because all of my competitors have one.'

Wrong answer. The blood, sweat, tears and cash you spend on creating an effective web site will be completely wasted if all you are trying to achieve is keeping up with the Joneses. Your web site must add value to your business, be in keeping with your brand image and portray your company or individual mission in the best possible way. If it's failing on any of these points, it's time to re-energise. A bad web site really is worse than no web site at all.

THE HOW

'Flashing graphics, funky design and edgy product reviews will mean everyone loves our site.'

Maybe – but maybe not. It's more important to work out how your web site is going to add value, showcase the brand and portray your mission to the world. By really understanding that simplicity and usability are the keys to an effective and profitable (both fiscally and intellectually) web site, you are halfway there already. Sometimes interactive graphics will add value, sometimes they won't. Never add a feature just for the sake of it – ask the question 'You, Flashing Button, are you really helping me achieve my goals?'

THE WHO

'Of course I know who my audience is. Duh!'

No you don't, not really. You may have a target audience that you hope to drive to the web site, but they won't be your only visitors. Whilst it's certainly correct to tailor your offering to your core base, you should also welcome accidental or exploratory visitors by making your site clear, visually pleasing and self-explanatory.

Finding out whether your current site successfully portrays your mission can be easily gleaned from your homepage – for more information, check out IDEA 22, *Is that it?*

Try another idea...

'*Furious activity is no substitute for understanding.*'
H.H. WILLIAMS

Defining idea...

'*Know thyself.*'
THALES

Defining idea...

3

WANT A PIECE OF ME?

Creating a web site that works makes the user think that your company, product or ideas work. They have subconsciously bought into you. In essence you are starting off on the right foot, as acquaintances if not friends, and this will allow you to convert your users to consumers far more easily – whether they be consuming your products, information or beliefs.

How did it go?

Q   We've been trying to define our needs but it's difficult because we are not just an e-commerce operation selling to consumers – we offer different products to the trade. How can we accommodate such a mixed offering?

A   That's fine. If you do have a mixed offering, make that clear right from the homepage. Spell it out for users – Click Here For Retail Orders. Click Here For Trade Orders. *Don't make them wander round your site looking for clues; they will get bored and leave.*

Q   Marketing insist that we only want a core audience to use our site. Are they right to want to tailor it specifically for one group?

A   To an extent, but it's a little short-sighted. What about visitors who are not interested in your offering yet, but may be in a few years' time? You still need to accept that these users will visit your site now and you need to engage them.

Q   Our sales manager is adamant that our message is very simple. We sell high-quality stuff, cheap. Are we missing something?

A   Well, does your site say this? You might have Sale, Cheap Prices *and other value statements all over the site; but is there anything to reinforce the quality issue? If not, consumers will think you're cheap – and nasty.*

4

2

Look at me!

Web site promotion should be the encouragement of the progress, growth or acceptance of you or your company. A perfect promotional web site will do all of these things; a bad one can be ruinous.

Attract your users with a slick, well-executed web site. Don't slap them in the face with a wet kipper.

YOU AND THE REST OF WORLD

Every Tom, Dick and Harry is trying to promote, sell, force their views, convert, inspire, turn on and sometimes steal from hapless users of the World Wide Web. To decide that you want no part in the madness is highly honourable, but not terribly bright. It really is a case of 'if you can't beat 'em, join 'em'. Promoting yourself, your product or your views on the web can be expensive and ineffectual, or it can be so viral and successful that you'll be overwhelmed with demand. But how do you rise above the clamour of the internet to ensure that your site shouts loudest – without puncturing eardrums?

How to attract users to your product or web site is a book in itself. What is vitally important is to ensure that, however you decide to drive traffic to your site, when

Here's an idea for you... **Think of your favourite drink – alcoholic or otherwise. If you were designing a micro-site for the producer, what messages would you want to convey. How would you promote that product and why? With the results, formulate a list of core messages – so 'not over fizzy' would become [competitive advantage] and 'tastes great on ice or straight' would become [expanding market]. Apply the same rationale to your own site – is there a message to be conveyed? Are you conveying it? Are you reinforcing it? If the answer is yes to all, you are on your way to creating the perfect promotional web site.**

Defining idea... **'When I took office, only high energy physicists had ever heard of what is called the World Wide Web...Now even my cat has its own page.'**
BILL CLINTON

those visitors arrive they find a well-organised, tempting display of tasty morsels, not a rundown, understaffed branch of Little Chef.

Web users, by and large, are promiscuous – they will use your site for only so long as it continues to please them. When they've had their fill (or enjoyed all you have to offer) they move on to the next site. It is in those short few minutes – or seconds, depending on your performance (noticing any parallels here?) – that you have the opportunity to hook them.

WHY PROMOTIONAL SITES WORK

The best promotional web sites are those that don't confuse. They are clear in their message about what they are promoting, whether that be an organisation (e.g. financial services), a specific product (e.g. a new drink) or a concept (e.g. druid baptisms). The site, no matter how large, is geared towards this one purpose, and no matter which page of the site your user visits, they understand.

You can still show depth and breadth within a promotional site, but this should not all be crammed onto the homepage. Let your navigational options guide the visitor to where they want to go and let users travel at their own pace.

WHY PROMOTIONAL SITES DON'T WORK

The worst promotional web sites are those that try to cram everything on the homepage. The site's owner feels that they are showcasing their entire offering; the visitor gets confused, panics and leaves. Commonly, a web site is full of claims reinforcing quality, excellence, excitement and professionalism – yet the actual site is slow, badly designed and poorly maintained. From this, the user will be quick to judge – the only thing being promoted is your incompetence. Not the desired effect.

There is a fine art to successfully presenting your offering on the internet. For more ideas check out IDEA 31, *Time please, gentlemen* and IDEA 17, *Less is more, baby.*

Try another idea...

One way to attract users is by search engine maximisation. Check this out in IDEA 39, *Message in a bottle.*

And another...

'Accustomed to the veneer of noise, to the shibboleths of promotion, public relations, and market research, society is suspicious of those who value silence.'
JOHN LAHR, theatre critic

Defining idea...

Q **We are in an industry with very large players who can spend far more on their web design than we can. How can we possibly compete with their level of spend?**

A *Good web design doesn't always mean high cost – work within your budget but make sure your message is clear. If people like what you're promoting, they'll use your services and tell their friends. If you don't promote well you'll lose out, and that's nothing to do with competitors having more money to spend.*

Q **We are promoting a completely new concept on our web site. Should we break with convention in the web site design too?**

A *You can be as original or zany in your concepts as you like, but there are still conventions that should be adhered to if you want people to notice your site and feel inclined to read on. Whether you let text or images explain the concept, the rules of promotion don't alter – explain to users what it is, let them contact you for more information and don't confuse.*

Q **We would love to advertise our products in our own way. Unfortunately the manufacturers dictate how their items are featured on our web site. Will this hinder us?**

A *It can be a blessing when a manufacturer dictates image sizes, colours and other specifications. Work with them on it. If they demand you only use their information (product details, images/logo etc.) then make sure they provide the graphics/text as they like it. They'll also be able to help you in the promotion of your site by advertising you on their site/literature as an approved retailer. So, although they might hinder or impede your overall design, they'll provide advice, resources and access to potential customers you wouldn't normally come across – all for using a specific Pantone or tagline within your web site.*

3

Selling ice to Eskimos

Selling on the internet needn't be like flogging a dead horse (though if there's a market...). With the right approach, you can sell effectively and efficiently.

When I visit your web site I want to be encouraged to spend my money, not run away as fast as I can crying for my mum.

THE HARD SELL AND THE WEB SELL

Although the promotion of information and the ability to share information across continents was the *raison d'être* for the World Wide Web, it wasn't long before capitalism made its presence felt on the internet. The boom years are certainly remembered more for the spectacular valuations placed on e-commerce sites than a sudden worldwide interest in reading the complete works of Jean-Paul Sartre online.

There is money, and a lot of it, to be made from selling online – from the bloke in a shed selling old records on eBay to the international behemoths like Amazon shipping millions of products. Transactional web sites have become popular so quickly because they help us cash-rich, time-poor wage slaves do what we want with the minimum of effort – and that is the key: you should reflect the reasons *why* shoppers want to buy from your web site through the functionality of the site.

Here's an idea for you...

If you can organise it, and assuming you're not a courier company, turn off the shipping charge for your products for one week. Don't advertise this fact, except maybe on your homepage, and monitor your stats. The likelihood is that your visitor numbers will rise only slightly (users passing on the good news to friends) – but look what happens to your conversion ratio (the number of visitors against the number of orders placed). I'd be very surprised if this didn't have an immediate effect. Whilst it might not be viable to have free shipping all of the time, you could revisit your pricing models to see if you can recoup the money by other means; or, if you offer free shipping during peak times only, you could determine whether the increase in order volume will negate the need to charge shipping.

TALKING TECHNOLOGY

There is a glut of web site packages now available that can allow anyone to design, create and maintain a fully transactional web site. The quality and price of these products varies widely, as does the number of options available to the user about how different you can make your site. Nearly all are templates, so whilst you can dictate, say, the colours and the font, you won't be able to alter how a product or a page appears. Off-the-shelf products do serve a purpose, but if your budget can stretch, I'd veer away from these products and use developers (in-house or third-party) to build your site. Whilst developers will also be using a template of sorts, they should be able to match your specifications far more easily than a boxed product. Using developers also means that you can scale up, fix bugs, alter information and maintain your web site far more easily than using a boxed-product helpline somewhere in Tennessee or New Delhi.

LOOKING AT YOUR COMPETITION

Competitive analysis is crucial if you are selling products online in competition with other companies. I don't think there's a single thing that can't be bought through the internet (somebody's soul, virginity and hand in marriage have all gone under the virtual hammer), so you'll have a competitor somewhere.

Check out their site and see how they promote their products. Test their order pipeline by placing orders (and why not check out their cancellation process at the same time?) and monitor how they communicate with you (as a customer, not a rival), their delivery time and their packaging. They have (presumably) chosen to do things their way for a reason – is their offering and service better or worse than yours?

If your web site is working well and you are selling well, be sure you are capturing all of your potential customers and protecting your brand. Check out IDEA 44, *You're in my manor now.*

Try another idea...

'*In the modern world of business, it is useless to be a creative original thinker unless you can also sell what you create. [Users] cannot be expected to recognize a good idea unless it is presented to them by a good salesman.*'
DAVID M. OGILVY

Defining idea...

'*It is better to have a permanent income than to be fascinating.*'
OSCAR WILDE

Defining idea...

11

How did it go?

Q **We have our own proprietary web site and we have a healthy number of customers, but why aren't they buying?**

A *If you haven't already, it's time to look at your 'order pipeline' – how many clicks are there from product to checkout? Even though you'll still need to capture all the information, try asking the same questions on one or two pages fewer. This will give your customers less chance of getting bored and pulling out of the sale.*

Q **Our customers are buying, but the average order value is low. What could be causing this?**

A *Up sell! If users are ordering one product from you, encourage them to order more. You must entice them with either a reduction on the price of the second item or a saving on the overall postage. Group related products together on the web site and refer users to other products that may interest them.*

Q **We have mimicked all of our leading competitors' features; we feel we offer just as good a service. What can we do to make customers come to our site?**

A *You have to offer something different to the consumer. If you are facing stiff competition you need to give people a reason to shop with you, especially if you can't compare on price or advertising spend. Offer more information about each product, use celebrity or even customer endorsements of products and take a different approach to product presentation – make the site more aspirational or 'exclusive', therefore justifying, in the mind of the consumer, the higher price.*

12

4

Licensed to sell

There's more to selling on the web than the ubiquitous 'for sale' sign. Customers will only buy from you if they think you're 'legit'. So show them you're trustworthy.

We desperately want visitors to our site to trust us and consume, but we have to win that trust. There are some simple tools that can be used to make them consume with trust...

WHO CAN YOU TRUST?

Web users are becoming ever more trusting and willing to try and buy from new sites, but they will be looking out for some indicators, from you, that this is a safe plan of action. Although ultimately you'll be judged on the quality of your web site and the information it contains (and, if you're selling, your service to the door and the quality of the end product), you can help put your visitor's mind at rest with some simple visual points of reference or anchor points.

Here's an idea for you... **Contact your local council and see if there is an online business initiative that you could be involved in. Although initially it may only be joining a list of local businesses in a web directory, it may lead to more in the future. See if they will endorse, certify or approve your site. It's all free advertising and another way to make your users feel safe.**

HOW SECURE IS YOUR SOCKET?

If you're selling across the internet, you'll already have an online payment processing solution for e-commerce merchants that allows your site to easily and securely accept and process credit card, debit card and purchase card payments (SSL encryption). But does your customer know this? It's essential that you reinforce the safety of your site whenever possible. Although bamboozling your customers with needless technical data may scare them off, a simple mention, both in your help pages and during the order pipeline (about the time you're asking for their card details), is both courteous and sensible.

COURTING CONSUMERS

Like them or loathe them, consumer organisations carry clout and influence the buying habits of the general public. Depending on your industry, there may or may not be a specific consumer organisation you could contact, but there are certainly generic groups that are worth getting into bed with.

If you can get a certificate or statement (usually a small graphic that can be added to your homepage) that shows an independent judge or panel has tested your site and is satisfied with how you operate, the user will immediately know that other *real people* have ordered from you before and have actually received goods for their cash!

SCRATCH MY BACK...

If your site is more community focused than commercial, there may be a web ring you can join. These are simply groups of sites with similar interests which agree to have reciprocal links. Although you may lose a few users when they follow the web ring link away from your site, you'll also be gaining users who likewise pass on to you.

You could contact the owners of sites that are similar to your own, but not competitive. If their information, services or products are related in some way, then mutual endorsement might prove beneficial. With the endorsement, the user will have greater confidence in the site they are visiting, and there will be a highly visible link to the related site.

YOU GOT A LICENCE FOR THAT?

If you have any relevant qualifications, awards or endorsements, shout about it. If your web site is offering users advice or information, spell out why your visitor should trust you (or give you money). If you're a doctor, mention it; if you have been operating for fifteen years (not surgically; the patient probably wouldn't survive), mention that. Have you been approved by a governing body? Do you have a licence to practise? Are you a member of a professional organisation?

For more about linking to others check out IDEA 45, *The missing link.*

Try another idea...

'*The only way to make a man trustworthy is to trust him.*'
HENRY STIMSON

Defining idea...

'*Put more trust in nobility of character than in an oath.*'
SOLON

Defining idea...

15

Defining idea...

'A person who trusts no one can't be trusted.'
JEROME BLATTNER

Spell it out for the user and let them see that you're no fly-by-night operation or self-styled guru (unless, of course, you are a self-styled guru!). Your web site is your CV and your waiting room – it should contain the same information as the user would expect to find in either (except maybe the ten year old housekeeping magazines).

COMMUNICATION BREAKDOWN

The old maxim 'treat others as you would expect to be treated yourself' really is true when it comes to communicating with your customers – especially if you are taking their money. Although you'll be sending out a receipt with the products, that could be in a few days or a few weeks. You must, if only out of courtesy, inform customers that (a) you have received their order and (b) their order has shipped (when applicable). Consumers are getting better at trusting internet retailers, but the thieves just find new ways to steal, cheat and embezzle. If you're expecting consumers to trust your company, at least confirm that you're legit, on the ball and contactable, by ensuring that your site (or, more accurately, the database) is sending out auto emails whenever an order is received/shipped. Cost of implementing: negligible. Cost of not implementing: lost orders, customers, goodwill, trust...

The same can be said for online forms. Even if it'll take you days or even weeks to answer the questions, acknowledge receipt of the email or online form with a simple courtesy auto email, thanking them for their question and promising a speedy response.

CAN I GET A RECEIPT FOR THAT?

It defies belief that any honest, supposedly reputable company operating above board can still be shipping orders to customers without the inclusion of an invoice/receipt for the products. Not only is this a legal requirement when selling goods or services, it's simply good manners. Although each country differs slightly, the general rule of thumb is that you should include the product or products that have been bought, the quantity, the price paid, any tax (VAT, state tax, etc.) incurred, a unique reference number, the date, your address and the buyer's address. It's really quite simple – and if you have a transactional web site, then this information is all being captured anyway. Provide the customer with it all, or face very expensive and possibly freedom arresting consequences.

'Do not trust all men, but trust men of worth; the former course is silly, the latter a mark of prudence.'
DEMOCRITUS

Defining idea...

How did it go?

Q   Our web site has only been operating for a year, but the directors want to give the impression that we've been around a lot longer. What can we do to give the impression that we are established?

A   *You don't have to specify years in business if you feel it's detrimental. Do include other information though about qualifications, awards, etc. Show how well qualified you all are, and why customers should feel confident and safe paying you money.*

Q   Marketing argue that joining a local business directory makes our company look a bit desperate. Is this the case?

A   *No it isn't. It looks like you're embracing your local community. Granted it may not lead to hundreds or thousands of new visitors, but it will raise your profile.*

5

We want information!

Information should be displayed on your web site clearly and concisely. Keep the waffle for breakfast.

Much like dressing up for the evening, wow onlookers with sheer simplicity and a neat composition — leaving the gaudy accessories and false eyelashes to the pretenders.

GETTING THE MESSAGE ACROSS, FAST

Slow-loading pages, whether the problem is at the server or client end, will limit your chances of hooking the user. Their patience will come to an end, abruptly, if their searches are in vain. Lead them to their destination with a simple interface, obvious options (buttons, links and choices) and a clear pathway. In a way, your web site should be like an airport runway – whilst there are escape routes off to the left and the right for slow-moving ground traffic, for the user who wants to fly supersonic, it should be straightforward and straight ahead.

SCAN-FRIENDLY TEXT

We don't read web sites the same way that we read books. Our attention will be grabbed (and distracted) by larger text, animation, images and certain words. You

Here's an idea for you...

Steve Krug, an American web usability expert, once wrote that you should take the text on your web site and cut the word count in half, and then cut it in half again. Obviously, this does not mean leaving...sentences...like... It means that you should look at condensing your text into short, snappy sentences that convey the same message without the padding. Web users are too busy, in too much of a rush and so easily bored that there isn't the time for fluffy sentence structure and long diatribe. Look at the text on your own homepage. Try the exercise and cut the text down to half, then try it again. It is difficult, but astonishing that the same messages and information can still be included. If you like the results, implement them on the site.

must recognise and respond to this. If some areas of your homepage are completely ignored by users, see it as valuable feedback about where your primary real estate really is. Monitor which links work and which do not, switch them around, and play with the size and the colour until there is a more equal spread of exposure across the page.

SEE BLUE FOR MORE INFORMATION

Using links as a dictionary, footnote, endnote or quotation source is a great way to ensure that your overall message reads well while indicating that additional information is available should the user desire it. Different users will have different levels of knowledge about you, your products and your information. It is a common mistake to tailor your message for the lowest common denominator, and explain everything in too much detail. Instead, assume the reader is very well informed. By doing so, the tone of your information will alter, and your reader will feel she is being treated as an equal rather than as a juvenile (unless, of course, your reader is a juvenile). If she does require more information, then she can click on the word/s to find out more.

SEEING RED

A trick sometimes used to pad out web sites is to repeat the same information in different areas of the site. Don't! There's nothing more annoying than hunting for information on a web site and re-reading paragraphs or entire descriptions on a page you haven't previously visited. It's just so annoying. Re-reading paragraphs. So annoying. This doesn't convince the user that you're a bigger and therefore more important web site. No, it confuses and annoys because we are left unsure if there is a third of fourth version of the text that may be more up to date than the information that we have just read, twice.

The layout of your web site, your navigational options and the language used on your site will greatly affect users and their interaction with your site. To read more, check out IDEA 14, *As clear as mud*.

Try another idea...

'Knowledge is of two kinds. We know a subject ourselves, or we know where we can find information on it.'
SAMUEL JOHNSON

Defining idea...

LACK OF OPTIONS

Although I urge short and snappy text, this is not to be confused with no information at all. Although your primary objective for your web site may be to sell products, or to provide information about a charity – this is not necessarily your visitor's main concern. It is imperative that you offer users the chance to find out what they want. This is usually achieved through a help page, a search box or a FAQ page. However you decide to show your information, be sure that it's all there. Although it will be difficult to second-guess every user about what they are looking for, be sure to include your contact details so that they can ask.

'Everybody gets so much information all day long that they lose their common sense.'
GERTRUDE STEIN

Defining idea...

How did
it go?

Q **Editorial insist that the information on our homepage is already as short and snappy as can be. What other alterations can we make to get the same effect?**

A *Try the exercise again using a product page or somewhere other than the homepage. Some of the copy will have been rushed or ignored for a long time. Fix it.*

Q **Our web site is industry-facing and therefore needs to have clear descriptions and contain lots of technical details. This is not something that can be jazzed up. What else can we do to improve our web site?**

A *There are some pages you won't be able to alter. However, it's still worth looking at the ancillary pages such as* Help, Contact Us, About Us, *etc., that could be changed from corporate monotone to contemporary chic.*

6

The acid test

Before going public, it's wise to test your web site on an unbiased third party. Find out the whys and wherefores.

Everyone has a view and some views are more useful than others; but everyone deserves to be heard. Yes, even that bloke from accounts who smells a bit.

THE TRUTH HURTS

User testing takes time. It can cost (but nowhere near as much as the cost of failure). Your testers' comments at best will make you angry and at worst will mean starting all over again, but, done professionally and at the right time, they can reap many rewards. User testing must go outside the walls of those with a vested interest in the success of the site. If you all share the same paymaster there is bound to be some bias, and that is not going to give you the honest and reliable feedback you need from Joe Public, the girl on the street with nothing better to do on a Tuesday afternoon.

When developing a new web site, or even just launching a new feature, if you have the network capabilities, launch the new build onto a staging or development server first. By hook or by crook get five non-company personnel in to test the site. Don't lead them with your questions; just set them a task and watch how they perform. Do listen to the comments about colour, layout, ease of use, etc. They all might focus on what may seem like a banal point – I don't really like that shade of green, looks a bit like suchandsuch.com, etc. – but this is what user testing is all about. It is by fixing the little problems that you will make your site great (as opposed to grate).

'**Man did not weave the web of life, he is merely a strand in it. Whatever he does to the web, he does to himself.'**
CHIEF SEATTLE

ACCEPTING FAILURE

It could be that your test site receives glowing reports from all concerned, and if so, great (what's your secret?)…but it's not very likely. There's always something overlooked – a broken link, some confusion over navigation, or a general dislike for the site's look and feel. Don't take it to heart; no design will ever be watertight – that's why you're testing in the first place. Far better for a handful of people after the breakfast news and before the children get home to expose the faults early in the project than to launch and have to firefight in full view of the public and your competitors.

WHAT IS YOUR NAME?

Testing can be done on a shoestring and anyone who knows what the internet is will do (anyone who thinks it's something to do with beach volleyball should be avoided at all costs). Prepare a brief for the testers. Introduce them to the company and the web site, and explain why you have engaged them. Set specific tasks, but don't set a time limit (these are real people trying to interact with your site; if they are slow, it's the site functionality to blame). Now sit back, relax and cringe.

It's painful watching users test a site, but it really reveals which areas still need attention. Be sure to test the site yourself immediately before you conduct a test – there's nothing worse than paying someone to look at 'page cannot be displayed'. Be sure to empty the cache so that all the links are fresh.

Making sure your users like using your site in a test environment is incredibly important – but so is keeping your site fresh and relevant for those users many months down the line. Check out IDEA 52, Sticky buns.

Try another idea...

WHEN THE PART IS GREATER THAN THE WHOLE

Different companies have different views about focus groups and their ability to truly test a web site. Personally I think focus groups are great when you want to try out a new advert or chocolate bar but absolutely dreadful at commenting on a web site and its functionality. Focus groups work for 'pedestrian' media – they'll either like your new logo or they won't. But when you're testing interaction, the group dynamic is actually counter-productive. Not only will you have Frank looking over the shoulder of Marge to see what she did; Simon will quickly nip off to Hotmail to read his emails and Helen will be placing an order with a competitor – all on your machines, whilst you're paying them! To see how a user interacts with your web site, you need to test a user on her own, with no distractions. By all means test a number of users over a day or week, but treat them like suspects in a police interview – don't let them meet or compare notes (and don't beat them!). Only when you have completed the testing should you then see what, if any, correlation can be drawn.

'All programmers are playwrights and all computers are lousy actors.'
UNKNOWN

Defining idea...

'What we have to do is to be forever curiously testing new opinions and courting new impressions.'
WALTER PATER

Defining idea...

Q   **Our testers were all obsessed with spotting typos and not testing functionality. How can we keep their mind on the job at hand?**

A   *You must explain what you are testing. If the text is just temporary window dressing, say so. Set the testers a specific task – try and buy a book written by Rhys Wilcox or download a document about rainforests. Alternatively, remove all typos first.*

Q   **The testers were reluctant to go through the order pipeline and buy products. Without testing the site from start to finish we feel the exercise won't give us the results that we require. What can we do to ensure that the testers are working towards the same goals as us?**

A   *The testers were quite right not to actually order products from you – they may not want to buy a lawnmower today! You must set up a dummy test credit card number (don't make it up, request one from your e-commerce payment handler) and let them go through the entire pipeline so that they see every page. You might also want to set up a dummy email address for the testers to use when placing orders.*

Q   **The testers said the site was perfect. Not a single complaint. Surely this means we have the ultimate problem-free web site?**

A   *You're telling fibs...or you paid them too much!*

7

Me, me, me!

Specialist and self-promotion sites don't necessarily follow the usual rules. So what rules do they follow?

Self-promotion starts with becoming a web-exhibitionist. Very soon you will have moved on from simply sticking out your tongue to pulling a full-on moonie.

With so many web sites all offering the same, or similar, it's the quirky specialist offerings that are receiving the column inches in the media. There's never been a better time to operate a specialist niche web site.

BREAKING THE LAW

As a direct contradiction to advice throughout this book, in the case of the specialist or self-promotion sites, you can break the rules of convention in terms of layout, language and navigation; in a way, that's the point. But whilst being quirky is great, you must still get your message across or else all will be in vain. There are some wonderful web sites out there – from the zany to the intense, from the scary to the bizarre. Many stem from one person's obsession with a certain subject, and from that passion is born the specialist web site.

Here's an idea for you... **Write down ten things that someone visiting your site may want to learn about you, your products or your company. Now look at your homepage. Are these ten reasons all addressed or at least available through the navigation? If not, you'll need to re-visit and re-energise your site. You only have one chance to hook your user.**

From pigeon racers to bell collectors, they are all out there in cyberspace like beacons to like-minded individuals around the world. Some of the sites are dreadful, some are fantastic and many make the mind boggle – but what do they all have in common? They are the manifestation of a passion realised through the internet.

If you do have a specialist site, don't be afraid to push the boundaries in terms of design, content and functionality. If your offering is truly unique, you have the advantage that no one else is out there doing the same thing. But there has to be a limit. Your users' tolerance levels may be much higher if they have hunted you down – in a way, we all take what we can get on occasion –

Defining idea... **'Sexually, we are all competing for the same seat on the bus and the thing that holds it together is the tightly held conceit that we are all sexual gods. How can I believe in my own uniqueness when there's a cat out there exactly the same as me?'** JEFF MELVOIN

but be warned, there is always someone else waiting in the wings to throw off their cloak of understudy and rise up to the challenge of lead actor. To remain truly specialist you have a duty to yourself, your company (or your cat) and your audience to keep your site fresh and updated.

Remember, a messy or out-of-date site does not reflect on the developer. It reflects on you.

It is important to constantly re-revisit your homepage and the site in general to ensure it's still current, viable and accomplishing your goals, check out IDEA 42, *Chained to the kitchen sink*, for more about good web site housekeeping.

Try another idea...

'Do not, for one repulse, forego the purpose that you resolved to effect.'
WILLIAM SHAKESPEARE

Defining idea...

Q My weblog (blog) is just about my thoughts on a wide range of topics, there's no way I can cover them all on the homepage. How can I possibly narrow the content down?

How did it go?

A *Depending on which weblog software you're running, you may be able to create a homepage that will allow you to categorise your posts under headings, as well as by date. Some visitors may be very keen to read your thoughts on politics but not on religion – if you can help them in their search you'll be gaining a reader.*

31

Q   **Our site looks great but it's impossible to get the third-party developers to update it. Won't moving to another development house or arranging for our hosting to take place in another location cost a fortune?**

A   *An out-of-date site is truly awful. Shop around for a hosting package that will either allow you to update yourself through hard code or WYSIWYG (What You See Is What You Get) software such as Dreamweaver. Or, find a developer who will update as you desire, or will agree to spend a set amount of time each month on your site. It is easy to change hosts, don't let anyone convince you otherwise.*

Q   **We are really unhappy with our web site. It has cost us a fortune and we simply can't afford to go through the process again. Do you have any advice for the terminally web-weary?**

A   *Development costs have come right down over the last couple of years and you can now pick up a professional, fast, easy-to-update site for a few hundred pounds if you shop around. There are even companies that specialise in creating web sites for certain professions, easily found through a search engine. By not updating your site you could be losing far more in terms of lost sales or visitors.*

8

Is that a swoosh, or are you just pleased to see me?

The need for instant recognition makes web branding an absolute necessity. Find out where to stick your logo for maximum effect.

Since we were kids we've identified with symbols; we'd mark schoolbooks with them, and the occasional bus shelter or loo — now older, you're still looking for a simple design that would grace any public convenience.

A POWERFUL DEVICE

If your company is already established, then the chances are you already have a brand name and a logo. How much you paid for this logo is knowledge that you'll probably want to take with you to the grave. It is a straightforward procedure making this device web friendly. If you're just toying with the idea of creating a logo, think long, hard and carefully about your decision. A logo in the real world will hopefully be an instantaneous visual image that is synonymous with your

Here's an idea for you...

Imagine that you're setting up as a rival to your own web site. You are free from the constraints of having decided on a company name already. You are looking for the most user-friendly, obvious, clever, self-explanatory brand name. What is it?

Now search to see if that web site is taken. If it's not, buy it immediately. Whilst it may never become your main URL, for the sake of some small change you now own a domain name which could prove very useful in the future – if not as your main site, as a route to test new products, run specific marketing campaigns or merely set to redirect visitors to the main site – either way, not a bad purchase. Who knows, if things go badly with your current employer, you could always become that competition for real!

company. This is no different on the web. The best example is e-commerce operations that not only brand their site, but reinforce the message with branded packaging materials – ensuring that not only the end-user but everyone who has anything to do with the delivery of that product is aware of the company (and to an extent the product/s contained within). A logo should be visually stunning, attention-grabbing and to some degree self-explanatory.

WWW.HOWAMIEVERGOINGTOREMEMBER THAT.COM

There is a lot to be said for having a short, snappy web address. Not only does it roll off the tongue better, it allows less room for error on the part of the user. Every letter is a potential spelling mistake, and every spelling mistake is a potential lost customer.

Choosing a name for the site that works for the company, that remains short and isn't confusing for customers, is time well spent. However, sometimes a company name simply isn't transferable as a web site address. This may be a difficult or easy decision to make, but it can make sense to alter the name of your site completely. In essence you're creating a new brand name or, if this is more palatable, a new internet sales arm.

Don't feel that your domain name has to be a proper name, or anything vaguely related to the name of the company behind it. This is all about marketing, exposure and design. If a made-up word makes some sort of sense, won't win you a triple-point-score in Scrabble but when you mention it people immediately know how to spell it – you're on to a winner.

There is also something to be said for having an internet brand that begins with one of the first five letters of the alphabet. Most directories, lists and results are categorised using the alphabet – it is, by and large, the fairest and most sensible way of doing things. Bearing this in mind, you can stack the odds in your favour by ensuring you're in the first few per cent of any list simply by using the letter A.

To learn more about navigation and the correct place to put what, check out IDEA 43, *Piss up & brewery*.

Try another idea…

'He who establishes his argument by noise and command, shows that his reason is weak.'
MICHEL DE MONTAIGNE

Defining idea…

'It pays to be obvious, especially if you have a reputation for subtlety.'
ISAAC ASIMOV

Defining idea…

NOW REPEAT AFTER ME

Your personal or company logo is the best anchor you can give to your users. Wherever they are on your site it must be visible, in the same place throughout. It must be a link – it is regarded as an industry standard that clicking on a logo will bring the user back to the homepage. Except maybe during the order pipeline, it should always be the same size and the same colour. Yes, it does feel like needless repetitiveness and it does take up valuable real estate, but it's that very repetition that your user expects and needs.

Being able to see the company brand no matter where they are in a site also acts as a visual reminder to your user that they are still within the same web site. This is especially important if you have a lot of mixed or third-party links and information on your web site. As soon as a user even feels that they have strayed into uncharted territory they may cancel their session.

'The new electronic interdependence recreates the world in the image of a global village.'
MARSHALL MCLUHAN

HANGING TO THE LEFT

If your web site is written in English then your logo should always be on the extreme left of the page. This is the area that the (English speaking) user's eye will always rest on first. English speakers read left to right, so placing your logo on the right is not going to help reinforce your brand, image or user confidence. There may be times to break from convention, but this is not one of them.

'**What the public wants is the image of passion, not passion itself.**'
ROLAND BARTHES

Defining idea...

Q **Everyone really likes the new domain name but marketing say that it's not feasible for us to re-launch under a new name. What will change their minds?**

A *For the time being, just buy the domain name and run a simple competition, or capture customer details through the new web site address. I assume that you're monitoring the hits, and the visitors are being redirected to your main homepage. It may become essential to re-invent your company at the new domain name in the future, and even marketing won't ignore the statistics – but for the time being, you now own it and nobody else can get there first.*

Q **Our CEO is worried that we will dilute our brand by having lots of different domain names. Is she right?**

A *Not if all the sites are singing from the same hymn sheet. No matter what the URL, if you or your company own it, it should have the same look, feel and logo as your main site/s.*

9
Are you listening?

Your web pages must be clear and easily understood. Your user should be in no doubt about what you have to sell or say.

It must be obvious to your visitor, as soon as they land on your web site homepage, exactly what is going on. It's no good saying 'Can you guess what it is yet...?'

DOES THE SITE DO WHAT IT SAYS ON THE TIN?

There are no warm-up laps with web site hits and there are few, if any, second chances. Your web site and the homepage in particular must project your core message. It has been known for the developers and those actually paying for a web site almost to come to blows over 'the look and feel' issue. Pretty, but impractical – or ugly and pragmatic? It's a difficult balance to get right.

TRICK BABY

There are two opposing schools of thought with regard to welcome messages on homepages. The decision is yours, but I think it's nice to acknowledge that somebody has made the effort to visit your web site out of the millions on offer.

Here's an idea for you...

If you're currently operating without a tagline, it's time to hit the thesaurus (and the flipchart and sticky notes, but leave the cat) and come up with the groundbreaking sentence that sums up your offering, ideology, mission, promise and style. If you're lucky you might have it cracked in a fortnight.

If you're already one step ahead and are using a tagline, is it still relevant today? Has your brand altered or your mission changed over the last few years? Reassess and imagine you have to create a brand new tagline. What would it be?

The rule of thumb is to keep your welcome brief, brief but welcoming. It is courteous to say hello, but this is valuable real estate you're using up. Introduce the user to your company or offering, but don't make them read an essay – there are other, more suitable parts of the site for that. What you need is a tagline.

TAG, YOU'RE IT

The user should instantly know what you're all about from the layout of the pages and the categories on offer in the form of the nav bar or buttons. Your brand or logo will be doing a great job in the top left corner, inspiring users to buy or read on. Telling them that you are the world's largest…whatever store or site is not going to inspire them much more – in fact, if it's their first visit and they've never heard of you before, it's only going to ask more questions of your integrity, history and value. Put simply, let the site design and the message/products do the talking and let others sing the praises of your company either in other media or as part of the testimonial section of your web site.

But you need a simple sentence, or set of words, that defines your company or your ideology. There are some very effective taglines out there, but there are also some dreadful attempts to be clever, witty or humorous that have failed miserably. A bad tagline will do you more damage than none at all.

BASKETS, BASKETS EVERYWHERE, AND NOTHING FOR ME TO BUY

If your web site is an e-commerce store, you haven't got time to mess around on the homepage. Forget about intros and a long soliloquy about why visitors should shop with you. Hit them with products immediately. Whether you decide to introduce the range of products or you just showcase your bestsellers is a separate business decision. Ensure that customers can choose a product from the homepage and start shopping. It is unlikely that visitors will all want to buy that exact product, but that's not why you're showcasing – you're making a statement that this site is an e-commerce store. *We Sell Things And We're Not Afraid To Say It.* If you've caught someone who's just looking for information, they'll move on, but the ones looking to spend money will be hooked. Now your nav bar comes into play, and the user will be able to browse around your site, knowing that they can buy anything on offer.

Taglines and branding go almost hand in hand. Check out **IDEA 8, *Is that a swoosh, or are you just happy to see me?***

Try another idea...

'A good listener is not only popular everywhere, but after a while he gets to know something.'
WILSON MIZNER

Defining idea...

'If I have ever made any valuable discoveries, it has been owing more to patient attention, than to any other talent.'
ISAAC NEWTON

Defining idea...

How did it go?

Q   Marketing are over the moon with our existing tagline and they can't see any reason to change it. How can I convince them otherwise?

A   *They might think that it's great, but do your users? If you have a way for visitors to leave feedback, or you mail your users, ask them to comment. It might turn out that your tagline is so witty and clever that only you understand it.*

Q   We've been trying to come up with a tagline for months. It's no good. Our offering can't be summed up in a single sentence. Surely this exercise does not apply to companies like ours?

A   *Ask your users to come up with ideas. If you're already enjoying visitors to your site and you have a vehicle for them to contact you, whether this is an online community, mail outs or even a simple feedback email address, run a competition. Web users are incredible at giving their opinion on anything, whether you ask them or not – harness this potential creative power and reward the winner with a few freebies (Ferrari, are you listening?). Make sure they sign away the copyright, though!*

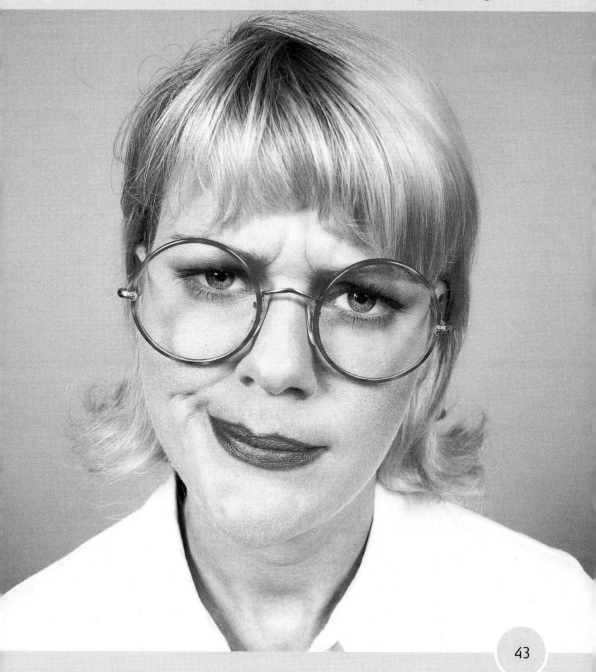

10

Sell out loser

Accepting advertising on your web site may bring in some revenue, but it could mean lost sales. Whatever the style, beware the pitfalls. Choose your path carefully...

The big question is: will you sell yourself for twenty pieces of silver?

SELLING OUT AND ENJOYING THE CONSEQUENCES

Accepting advertising, and the revenue that hopefully comes along with it, can be likened to selling your soul (or the soul of your site) to the devil. It can certainly bring in a huge amount of capital hitherto unavailable to you simply by adding a few banners and then sitting back and doing nothing. But you need to be sure that the benefits you receive in terms of cash, and maybe kudos through association, outweigh the dilution of your own site.

A SITE FOR SORE EYES

If capitalism is the overpowering reason why the internet took off and became so mainstream, so fast, then marketers are the field marshals of the army that made it happen. There are a number of ways that advertising can work on your web site which are discussed below, but all of them – no matter how unobtrusive – will,

Here's an idea for you...

If you do accept advertising on your site then there is probably a business need for that revenue. However, if advertising is something that you have never considered, try it for a short term, maybe a month. Monitor your hits and where your users go. Hopefully this experience will put you off the process forever!

without a shadow of a doubt, impact your site visually. Quite simply, the more an advertising campaign impacts, the more you'll be rewarded. The homepage is king in terms of des-res placement and top of the page is the big daddy compared with being hidden in areas of the site even your own staff wouldn't dare venture.

GOING DOWN?

Who you associate with is as important as what you get out of the deal. If the decision to lose your advertising virginity was a hard one, the decision about whom you let advertise is even larger. The power, brand, fame (and infamy) and reputation of your advertising partner will reflect on you. The knock-on effects of what a company has done in the past or might do in the future will affect how users view your site. If you decide to get into bed with a company involved in unethical practices, then you'll lose users who feel strongly about that cause.

Ensure that you have a contract with your advertising partner. Explain that you're happy with their reputation as it stands at the moment, but you must insist on a 'get-out clause' should those circumstances change – if they are being taken to court or receive negative press, for instance. Don't let yourself be dragged down with them.

FLASH, HE SAVED EVERY ONE OF US

Except when web sites started using this most annoying of advertising banners.

For more about giving users choice and not confusing them, check out IDEA 25, *Run away!*

Try another idea...

Flashing animation is not eye-catching in the sense that your user will be so impressed with the display that they will pledge a percentage of their earnings to both you and your advertiser for the next ten years; it's more in the sense of a sharp stick. It can cause immediate irritation and lead to long-term hatred.

I'm amazed that a large proportion of web sites that accept flashing banners are mainly text-based sites – information sites, community chat sites, etc. So the users go there to involve themselves in some text-heavy activity such as reading or writing posts – meanwhile, off to the right, or at the top of the page is an annoying banner offering a chance to arrange a new credit card, win millions or meet a Thai bride. Er, I don't think so!

Of all the advertising streams available to you, choose flashing animation as a last resort. It won't do your site any favours at all and I doubt whether is really works for the advertiser.

'Never go to excess, but let moderation be your guide.'
CICERO

Defining idea...

CPM

Marketers have their own lingo for web advertising that is incredibly straightforward but can confuse the uninitiated. CPM stands for Cost Per Thousand. Yes, thousand begins with a T not an M – but not in Latin. For some bizarre reason we use the Latin M to represent one thousand clicks in the case of measuring clicks.

'Advertising may be described as the science of arresting the human intelligence long enough to get money from it.'
UNKNOWN

So, a web advertising deal will often be expressed as a financial value paid for every thousand clicks the banner or ad receives. This is usually monitored by the advertiser (through a referrer address), but it doesn't hurt for you to monitor it too.

CPC

CPC is a little more straightforward – Cost Per Click – so rather than waiting for one thousand hits, you'll receive something for every referral you give to an advertiser.

Every deal is different, so there is no need to get worried if your advertiser insists on CPC over CPM or visa versa. Work out what each hit means to you in fiscal terms and work out how much traffic you'll drive to their site.

Usually, your deal will be based on CPM when you're driving traffic to the advertiser's homepage. CPC will be used when you're driving traffic to a specific page or area of the advertiser's site.

FIXED FEE

Unless the money offered is astronomical (which is highly unlikely) or you're agreeing to the advertising on moral grounds and cash is not your motivation, never take a fixed fee for allowing advertising on your site. Quite simply, there is no way to monitor how effective the advertising is, so you might be diluting your site for virtually nothing, with no gain for yourself.

Q   **The finance department thinks that advertising, done properly, works fine for our site and makes us money. In fact, they would rather we seek to increase the number of advertising partners we have. Can this be a problem at all?**

How did it go?

A   *Good to hear that advertising is working well for you. I'm not totally down on advertising as it can prove to be a very lucrative revenue stream. But do choose your partners carefully and try, if you can, to be subtle. By not controlling the advertising you run the risk of confusing your own offering and putting users off from visiting your site.*

Q   **A firm approached us offering to provide a steady stream of advertisers for our site. Is there a catch?**

A   *Probably not, other than losing a portion of the revenue as a 'finders fee'. These firms can be very good at ensuring that the space on your site you have earmarked for advertising is constantly filled. You should still have control over which companies are featured and the quality of the adverts shown.*

11

Guilty until proven innocent

Web sites are governed by national and international laws. Know what they are and how they affect you. Be aware; be very aware.

You can flirt all you want with the law (there are some very frustrated paralegals out there who will thank you for it) but its long hand won't feel nice on your shoulder!

There's more to selling than taking cash and sending goods; and posting articles and information on the internet is not so simple. There are laws in place governing your web site, both in your country and those where the content might be read or you ship products to. Ignoring your legal obligations is foolhardy and dangerous.

PUBLISH AND BE DAMNED

You can't simply write something about Mr X unless it's true, and, should he take exception to your scribblings, more often than not you'll have to prove that it's true rather than Mr X prove that it isn't. No matter how strongly you feel or how badly you think that you have been treated, publishing libellous statements on the internet is no different than publishing them in a book or magazine. You will be taken to court, it will be very expensive if you are in the wrong and it will be a

Here's an idea for you...

If you don't have legal pages on your web site, this must be addressed immediately. Assuming that there is already a statement of some description on your site, find out when it was last updated. Does it cover your contractual agreement with users and their agreement when using your site? Is it clear who owns the copyright of the text, images and other content found on your site?

It is well worth the cost of having a legal expert read over, if not create, your statement. Pinching another web site's statement and altering it to suit you own needs is not good enough – you'll be caught out either by the originator or by a user finding loopholes.

painful experience – all because of hasty typing. If you are posting information on your web site, check and re-check it before going live.

IT WASN'T ME!

If you are selling products built by a manufacturer, or you are posting comments, news or information that you or your company did not create, you must include a disclaimer on your site explaining your arrangement with third-party suppliers. This won't dilute what you're selling or posting; it's a simple explanation that content is drawn from various sources and, therefore, you can't be held responsible for misinformation, errors, omissions or the views of suppliers. This is not cowardice; it's your responsibility as an aggregator of data, and your protection should things goes horribly wrong.

BATTERIES NOT INCLUDED

Most countries now empower their citizens with statutory consumer rights. Statutory rights differ wildly from country to country, but fundamentally all customers have a right to receive the product they paid for, to receive a product free from defect and to return it if it does not perform to their expectations. If you are a bona fide retailer, this should not be viewed as a problem. If the goods are faulty, then you have a case to raise with the manufacturer or supplier. If the goods are not as advertised, then you need to adjust the information available on your web site. If the customer received a completely different item than that ordered, then you have a problem with your supply chain. All of the problems a customer might find with your service or products are faults that need to be addressed by you.

IN GOD WE TRUST

Many people do, but when tempers start flaring you need a more mundane court of law to decide any serious disputes between web site and user. Specify under which laws you or your company are operating. If there is a dispute, which country's law will govern the proceedings? It is absolutely paramount that you include on your web site contact and company details (if applicable), and explain the contract you and the consumer are entering into when they view/download/buy/quote/steal images from your site. Leave nothing out and constantly revisit your legal pages to ensure that they are still 'legal' and up to date.

Knowing what to include in your legal statement is not that straightforward. You need to re-visit and fully understand the actual purpose of your web site to ensure that you are addressing the specific requirements of *your* dedicated legal document. For more about getting back to basics check out IDEA 1, *Knowing me, knowing you, a-ha.*

Try another idea...

'*A man cannot be too careful in the choice of his enemies.*'
OSCAR WILDE

Defining idea...

'*The problem with any unwritten law is that you don't know where to go to erase it.*'
GLASER and WAY

Defining idea...

53

I'VE ONLY BEEN ONCE, BUT I STILL HAVE RIGHTS!

Users, whether they are accidentally 'just looking' or hard-core fans of every one of your web pages, have rights. Thankfully, for those of you selling products, your users tend to make decisions such as accepting cookies at browser level, which means, if you want to, you can leave cookies on their browser to personalise content and 'help' them come back to relevant pages in the future. Add a disclaimer if your web site points to any other site or source of content on the web. This includes links to friends or associate company web sites. If you have no control over their content you should make sure that you are not held responsible for what they do wrong.

How did it go?

Q **We don't sell through our web site and there's no need for us to post a legal statement about the content. Surely this idea doesn't apply to us?**

A *Your web site must have something on it, whether it's a single image or a paragraph of text. The least you can do is show who the copyright owner is, otherwise the content is public domain.*

Q **We are a very small company and can't afford legal representation. Editorial have written something that reads like a legal document. Will that do?**

A *If you can't afford to pay a legal expert to look over your text for an hour or so, then you are unlikely to be able to afford a lawsuit or a court case that might occur if you have got it wrong. Take the hit and see the process as just as important as that of creating your logo or mounting an advertising campaign.*

12

Pretty flash, but do they make you run faster?

Given that you have only a few seconds to attract a visitor's attention and convert her into a consumer, is there really any excuse for forcing people to watch a Flash intro?

Be careful when investing money in Flash — he may have saved every one of us, but all people remember is that bad hairdo! Spend your money elsewhere.

MAKING A POINT

Whenever a new technology becomes mainstream, or more accurately, when a new fad becomes apparent, everyone jumps on the bandwagon. One minute static homepages were all the rage (well, actually, that was all that was available) and the next minute to not have a Flash intro put your web site into the dark ages. This is a classic case of web designers trying to keep up with the Joneses. Don't jump onto the bandwagon unless there is a definite business reason to do so.

If you currently 'enjoy' a Flash intro on your web site, consider changing it back to a static homepage. Don't worry, the intro can be saved and played back to customers, but let them choose if and when to view it by offering it as an option through the navigation of your homepage. During the time that the intro is turned off, monitor your hits and see (over the course of a few days) whether the number of users clicking on your homepage continues through to other pages on your site. If you are unable to monitor this, see if the number of downloads, sales or comments increases in the time that the intro is turned off.

HOW BIG IS YOURS?

No matter what the set-up is at your place of work, you must always build for the lowest common denominator. Although by 2010 broadband internet (128 kps+) will be the absolute minimum, until then, you must cater for people using carrier pigeons and rickshaws for their internet connection. Give peace (of mind) a chance: offer your users the option of skipping the intro if they wish and let them jump straight to the money – in this case, your homepage. Otherwise, the intro you have spent so much time designing, implementing and enjoying through your 3 Meg pipe will be wasted on us ignorant internet cave dwellers who only popped by for a cup of ice and to see whether you would be happy to accept a sack of fruit for a morsel of your tasty mammoth.

ENOUGH ALREADY

'I've got through the download of your intro and I enjoy what you have to offer me. I haven't got problems with the speed, it's all working fine, but I have got a life outside of the internet and now I am bored. Really bored. Intros can work; they can impress and they can inspire, but what next? I was happy to sit through about 30 seconds of corporate design-tastic spiel, but when is this nonsense going to finish? If you insist on an animated intro, be sure to include information about how far I am into the download and more importantly, how far I am into the playback. I am a consumer and my tolerance is low.'

For more about enticing your user from the outset and getting them hooked and involved in your site, check out IDEA 48, *I'm a believer.*

Try another idea...

GONE IN 60 SECONDS

I can't stress enough that your time to entice new and existing users is limited. While a small percentage of the internet population will be won over by your 'bling bling' animation, the vast majority of us want some substance. 'Time is money, baby, and no matter how sweet your intro, if I am not feeling sustained I will simply move on. You have got about 60 seconds to really do it for me, and by adding an intro to your offering you are only eating into your own time.'

TO INTRO, OR NOT TO INTRO

The Jesuits are keen to influence children while they are still young to ensure that they have faith for life. Surely the same is true with regard to internet users?

Nonsense. The only organisation that should design and install a Flash intro for their web site are those companies that are offering to build them for others. You won't capture the hearts and minds of your user by overpowering them with great graphics and fear of damnation. True conversion is only achieved by either performing a miracle or by delivering on what you promise. I would (usually) choose the latter path personally, but take care. Play with Flash and you'll get your hands burnt.

'Someone's boring me. I think it's me.'
DYLAN THOMAS

Defining idea...

'The secret of being boring is to say everything.'
VOLTAIRE

Defining idea...

How did
it go?

Q **The developers insist that our intro is design perfect, runs fast and completely defines what it is our company stands for – our web site simply wouldn't be the same without it. Could they be wrong?**

A *We all get attached to our technology and there are very many Flash intros that are absolutely stunning. But there is a time and a place for everything, and hitting people with the dessert before they've even tasted the starter is going to leave an odd taste in the mouth. Unless the entire web site is built to the same standard, you're going to raise your user's expectations and fall short of the full delivery.*

Q **The developers say, 'No! Our web site has just as much, if not more to offer, as the intro; we are merely showing them the tip of the iceberg and there are surprises still in store. In our particular case it makes much more sense to retain the intro.' So why should we change the site?**

A *You're lying! Or if you aren't, you're misguided by your developers' ego or your own. You simply cannot sustain great design with total accessibility – you are losing more customers and custom than you're gaining. Work on delivering good navigation and a good service before trying to con people with a flashy intro. Your visitors are your bread and butter – don't try to give them the cream without something sustainable to back it up.*

13

Smart cookie

Is it obvious what your buttons and links are? Is there a pattern thoughout your site? How is your visitor going to react if even you don't know where to go next?

Taking the time to spit-polish your buttons and make them as clear and legible as possible will win the customer over, promise. Even your mum'll be proud.

A SMART JACKET NEEDS SMART BUTTONS

Don't re-invent the wheel when it comes to designing buttons, unless there is a very, very good reason to do so. Yes, for the experienced web user, rolling a mouse over a word or an image will reveal whether something is clickable (the cursor will change from an arrow to a pointing hand), but why make the user, your customer or reader, think about it? Make it as obvious as possible that a button is a button. Of course diversification is good, and your design or concept for buttons may eventually supersede the existing industry standard, but probably not. Don't place more barriers in front of the user; use the tools that they are familiar with, in the style that they are familiar with. Buttons can still end up being funky – between colour options, shadowing, rollover graphics and sound effects, yours can be a novel approach without having to re-educate.

Here's an idea for you…

Choose a random page on your web site and count as many links as you can in two seconds. Now look at the same page in your own time and count how many links there really are. Which links came to your attention first, and why? Chances are they were highlighted in bold, or a different colour. Look at fixing the remaining links.

Choose a competitor or large e-commerce site and run the same exercise on their homepage. Are you able to spot more links in the two seconds? If you can, you've got it wrong and they will win customer loyalty; if you can't, then you already have competitive advantage.

A CHAIN IS ONLY AS STRONG AS THE WEAKEST LINK

It doesn't stop with buttons either. If a link is a link, shout about it. Don't be too subtle and expect users to hunt around the page for something to shoot at with their trigger finger (there are specialist sites for that); the mouse is a weapon and we're all very keen to rifle our way through your site, so let us. For example, if your base text is in black, highlight links in, say, blue and those that you have already clicked on in pink. Net result – you can scan the page quicker, take in the information and immediately know where you want to go to next. If I am still here hunting for an escape route I will be quickly losing my goodwill and patience with your site.

This is a point often overlooked in the design of a web site and more often than not goes back to an oversight on behalf of the developer. Whilst the murky red/brown/purple of a link previously used does injure the aesthetics of a web page, a used link should still be highlighted in a different colour. Users like and need to know where they have travelled before during that session (even if it might appear obvious to you). 'Tricking' them into re-visiting the same place again, even if unintentionally, will leave them frustrated and possibly angry with your site – a reaction that is hardly going to inspire them to buy or read much more. Used links for many users act like waypoints, 'This is a site I am unfamiliar with, here is a new page, but I can already see that I have visited some of the links before.' Familiarity with your site sets

If you want to learn more about the importance of allowing your visitor free reign to travel at will throughout your site, see IDEA 25, *Run away!*

Try another idea...

in and the customer feels free to continue surfing without fear of treading over old ground or fear that the little trail of breadcrumbs is going to be eaten up – leaving them stranded and alone, and far more likely to return to a web site that's more like home in Kansas and less like a gingerbread house in the woods inhabited by a cannibalistic witch...

Conventional sites don't have to be boring. Your site can still offer something different in terms of layout, use of colours and 'value-added' celebrity names or endorsements, sound,

'Only a fool doesn't judge by appearances.'
OSCAR WILDE

Defining idea...

images and writing style. But a link should always look like a link – a device that is clickable. There must be a nav bar somewhere apparent and you must offer the user the chance to 'escape' back home, available on every page, should they wish.

If your web site is an e-commerce store, then as well as offering users the chance to return home at any stage, the same must be said for offering them the chance to purchase by showing the shopping basket or cart icon on every page. This should make complete commercial sense, but you would be surprised at how many e-commerce sites don't keep the shopping basket as a permanent feature at the top of the page.

How did
it go?

Q   Our site is text based rather than product based, and links are used to explain definitions rather than to sell items. What's wrong with this approach?

A   *This is fine, but is it clear that you can click on specific words to find out their definition? If not, add instructions at the top of the page to explain this facility.*

Q   We saw most of the important links in the two seconds, so what's the problem?

A   *The problem is this – what is important to you is not necessarily what is important to your user. Let them decide what their priority is and give each link a chance!*

Q   Our developer says we should use text-based buttons rather than graphics. Are they right?

A   *Yes. Clever developer! Text-based buttons load faster and are easier to alter and add to, should you need to. The same rules apply, however. Make sure your text-based buttons are obviously clickable and the buttons visited leave a trail.*

14

As clear as mud

You only have a couple of hundred words to convey your message. Keep it clear, precise and to the point. Choose your words carefully.

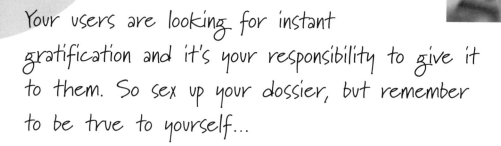

Your users are looking for instant gratification and it's your responsibility to give it to them. So sex up your dossier, but remember to be true to yourself...

CLEAR AND PURE

Coupled with the fact that you only have a limited number of seconds to 'hook' the user to your offering, you only have a few sentences to get that message across. Therefore, you must ensure that your site makes logical sense as well as grammatical sense. Would you want to buy a book from a shop with misspelled posters, or sports equipment from a store that fails to categorise your favourite team in the right league? No. Nor would I.

Here's an idea for you... **Look at your homepage carefully and give yourself a few seconds to see what parts/words/images catch your eye first. Now scroll to the bottom of the page and look at what you have left. If a user were to come across this part of your homepage first, would it be as apparent what the web site was trying to achieve? Your users will come to you through many different links and references, and sometimes by sheer luck alone. Wherever they land on your site it must tell the story. Scan your web site for black holes and ensure that they fit with the rest of the site.**

WELL-CRAFTED TEXT OR BLURBS ARE PARAMOUNT

Web sites should convey a message as quickly and painlessly as they can. Do not allow your writers the opportunity or free rein to practise flowery prose and personal diatribe about how wonderful they think your product or service is – let others sing your praises. Your writers should earn their pay through clear, crisp and engaging text. Blurbs should be teasers and no more. Let the image of the product, reviews or further information convince them that this information is good. A blurb needs to be like a dagger – short and to the point.

ORDER IN CHAOS

Bear in mind that despite years of practice at reading from left to right, as you are doing right now, we don't read web pages in the same manner. Although there are many rules to be gleaned from printed text, and newspapers in particular, one thing to note is that your reader won't be reading everything in the order that it is laid out. Instead of the usual left to right, or even top to bottom, we weave our way across a web page, erratically – attracted by certain words, buttons or images. Your user is scanning for information and there is no real logic behind how their eye is jumping – therefore, break everything up into clearly delineated sectors. Break lots of text with an image or a heading and give people links to move on. They want to taste you in 'bite size' pieces, so be as palatable as you can (less is morsel).

SAY IT HOW IT IS

The temptation to waffle is strong, but resist it with all your might. Padding a web site with useless information is more transparent on the internet than it is on any other medium. We will tolerate time wasting on the TV, in the newspapers, on the radio and especially during football matches – but on 'my time', surfing the web, I want the synopsis. Tell them what you are going to tell them, tell them and tell them again (but don't repeat yourself). By the time you have done all this, there isn't much time left to do anything else.

Getting your point across quickly is the essence of web sites. Getting it right can be hugely rewarding; getting it wrong is suicide. For more about conveying a message effectively, check out IDEA 5, *We want information!*

Try another idea...

Writing good text for web sites is covered in more depth in IDEA 17, *Less is more, baby.*

And another...

'Freedom is just chaos, with better lighting.'
ALAN DEAN FOSTER

Defining idea...

'A life lived in chaos is an impossibility...'
MADELINE L'ENGLE

Defining idea...

How did it go?

Q **Surely, if people are used to the layout of a newspaper, it makes sense to copy what is familiar. Is it not right to follow the newspaper format completely?**

A *To an extent this is true, but you are not printing on paper and you are not printing news. Every medium is different and the web is no exception. There are conventions but not rules.*

Q **We use a software package to upload our web pages; the technical manager does not have control over how the items or sections are displayed. What can we do to be different?**

A *If you are not happy with the look and feel of your site, you should change your software or better still invest in a brand new web site designed and developed by a developer. You'll spend more, but you'll get the desired effect.*

Q **Our web site has a specific audience in mind. The directors are keen that we stick to those conventions and not the conventions of the web. Are they right to think like this?**

A *If you are on the web then you must confirm to web rules, no matter what your web site is offering. Even practitioners of your art or believers of your system or buyers of your products are also general web users. They won't think less of you for 'selling out'; they will simply know, intrinsically, what to do next.*

15

Looking good tonight!

Both text and images are important in getting your message across – but so is their layout. Here are some tips to avoid a tip.

Remember, subtlety is the best way into a woman's/man's (delete as appropriate) heart and a customer's wallet...

CREATING THE LOOK

It is the whole composition of the site that will etch itself into the mind of your users. No matter how well written your text is and no matter how eye-catching your images, if the content is presented badly it will fail to impress and will dilute the quality of your offering. In much the same way as a good painting requires a good mount and frame, a good web site must have a pleasing background, make good use of colour and be displayed in a professional font. Get all of this right and it will add value to your site, regardless of the quality of the content.

CHOOSE YOUR FONT, SIR

We all have a font that we are fond of. However, many fonts that look great on the printed page look dreadful on the screen. Prepare to compromise with your

On a staging or development server, take a couple of your web pages, choose a couple of colours that you don't currently use as well as some random colours you wouldn't ordinarily think of using in a million years and let your techies run riot. Ask them to be as zany and creative as they can and see what happens.

The end product will be a little bit scary and little bit different, but just look how a couple of colour changes alters the entire feel of a web site. It may not lead to finding a better composition than you have now, but it's a quick and easy way to find out if you can improve your look. And it might just go great in the spare

'**Never express yourself more clearly than you are able to think.'**
NIELS BOHR

developers. A good font is only good if it is legible. Make your suggestions and let them make theirs – look at actual web pages on a monitor to make your decision, not a print out (and only then overrule them!).

JUST A HINT OF APPLE

Personally I would recommend using primary colours only when you have to. Just as having too much on a page is noisy, primary colours are very loud; many users see primary colours as an admission of failure – the content isn't very good, but if I shout it out something might stick. Time to pretend you are painting the kitchen and use some Pantone cards to decide on which slightly off-cream background you are going to use. Remember, primary bad, pastels good.

CLICKABLE ICONS

As well as using colour to highlight that a link is indeed a link to another web page or web site, there are many typographical ways to enhance or reinforce the clickability of a certain word. The obvious and most popular solution is to highlight links in bold. Or you can increase the font size. Some web sites make their links italic, but I feel that this makes the word harder to read on the screen. What is only beginning to be used to great effect is to change the font of a link to help draw attention to the fact that you can click and go.

SHHH! THIS IS A LIBRARY, NOT A MONKEY HOUSE

It is of paramount importance to keep noise to an absolute minimum. One of the pitfalls of having multiple product managers all fighting for their product or service to be highlighted on the homepage is compromise. If you are ultimately responsible for what is loaded onto your homepage, give no quarter. If the limit is four products, or six news articles or whatever, stick to it and enforce some sort of rotation schedule. Compromise is disastrous. Letting everyone have a little bit of the page means confusion, noise and a murky picture for the user. A busy homepage does not mean that everything gets a fair share of the user's time and interest – everything loses out, as a messy page suggests a messy company. Be strict, be fair and wear a crash helmet.

Try another idea...

Tackling colours and fonts is only half the battle. No one will want to read your web pages unless there are a few images to complete the 'picture'. For more about using images on the web check out IDEA 18, *Red eye and open mouths*.

Defining idea...

'Clarity of mind means clarity of passion, too; this is why a great and clear mind loves ardently and sees distinctly what it loves.'
BLAISE PASCAL

Defining idea...

'Art is science made clear.'
JEAN COCTEAU

How did it go?

Q **We are limited in the colours we can use on the web site because our brand was created long before the internet ever existed. We simply can't change our colours now. Will this mean our web site will fail?**

A *Granted the logo might have to remain the same, but the internet is a discrete medium and therefore different rules apply. Your customers will still trust you if your site is built with a different look and feel to your printed material – in fact, they would much rather it was legible and pleasing to the eye than confused and fussy just because you insist on yellow text on an orange background.*

Q **How will we know which colours work best for us? Our developers usually deal with those sorts of decisions. Should we be dictating to them?**

A *If you are paying for the project, then it is your decision, not theirs. They might have their preferences and suggestions – listen to them, they will probably be right – but also ask for the site in a number of formats. Insist on a selection of fonts and colours to choose from.*

16

Style queen

House rules ensure consistency throughout a web site. No matter where in your site a user is, it should be obvious that it is your site, not some random part of the internet.

Create and maintain an identity always — shout out your company name until you are blue (or any other colour) in the face.

TYPOGRAPHICALLY SPEAKING

Those people who were first responsible for creating and adding content to your web site are usually the cause, albeit unconsciously, of the house style you are using today. No matter what format content for your web site is submitted, it all must conform to your house style, and that usually means someone altering it – even if that means inputting it onto the web site so that the font, size and paragraph formations fall into the pattern dictated within the HTML code. Point size is often overlooked by web site designers because, by nature of their job, they are used to looking at web sites all day. Although users have the ability to alter the resolution of their screen, choose a point size that is fair to the content and the reader.

Here's an idea for you...

Boring as it may sound, even if there are only one or two people responsible for updating your web site, create a set of rules. List the fonts you use, point size, the specification of images, word limits for product descriptions, editorial rules such as the use of hyphens and em dashes, suitable language, banned words and any editorial peculiarities your web site may have. This may all seem very obvious to you, but that should only make it easier to construct the document – and it will prove invaluable for the company should you or the other staff that update the site move on.

WHAT YOU SAYIN'?

Unless of course you are selling or promoting technical products or services, avoid techie terms like the plague. Acronyms like ISP, ASP, JAVA and even HTML can bamboozle your audience and scare them. If you must use technical terminology (such as in the help pages or legal page of your site), explain what it means. Do not assume that your audience is as well versed in the lingo as you and your company are.

BELOW THE FOLD

This is a term used in newspaper publishing to determine which articles are placed at the top of the page and which should appear lower down, or below the fold. As with newspapers, you must imagine your page as sections of real estate. The prime positions are those on the homepage. Within the homepage there is also the decision about what information, or products, takes pride of place. This decision will be one fraught with disagreement and politics, especially if your web site is multi-product, as each product manager will want to see their products in pole position all of the time.

Look at the newspapers for inspiration about the best way to use space on a page. Simple borders work best (they can be made up of space as much as physical lines). I never thought that I'd use the word apartheid in a

For more about how to approach layout on your web site check out IDEA 22, *Is that it?*

Try another idea...

positive way, but you must segregate your sections. Make it clear where one area begins and another ends. Use headings that are bolder or larger than the accompanying text, use space effectively and give the top of the page absolute priority. As a general rule use a triumvirate approach for each product, section or point you wish to show – a heading, an image and a blurb. But most importantly, once you have decided on a format, keep it. Make sure it is the same throughout the site – once people get used to your layout and understand what is required to navigate, they don't want to be confused again. Define, from an early stage of development, your own house style.

SCROLLING ALONG

Sad but true, some web users are not aware of scrollbars and their function. The net effect: anything below the fold is never seen, ever! So choose what fills your top spaces carefully. Yes, it is a prime position for selling your best or latest offering, but it should also be used to show products or information often hidden within the depths of your site.

'Never offend people with style when you can offend them with substance.'
SAM BROWN

Defining idea...

'Without an acquaintance with the rules of propriety, it is impossible for the character to be established.'
CONFUCIUS

Defining idea...

75

How did it go?

Q **We're not that rigid in our approach. Our writers write what they want then FTP it across to the site. Why should we change?**

A *There's nothing wrong with numerous people having the ability to upload live to your web site – but that doesn't mean that you can't insist on them adopting a set of rules. Making it clear from the outset will make it less embarrassing if you have to remove their content at a later date.*

Q **Our site is specifically for users to post comments about whatever they want. They won't tolerate us telling them how to write. How can we protect the consistency of the site without stepping on too many toes?**

A *You're not telling them how to write, you are instructing them on how best to show off their writing. By ensuring you have consistency throughout the site, it means your users (their readers) will be more likely to read more pages – once visitors become familiar with a house style they become more comfortable spending time on your site.*

76

17

Less is more, baby

Web language has its own style and form – it's short, sharp and snappily dressed. Learn how to write effective copy for the web.

Writin' propa, in'it — not that difficult, blood. Get down with those crazy kidz.

Language is a beautiful thing; we have a whole dictionary of words and we have always been told to take our time explaining things with them. Then along came the information superhighway to add to our busy-busy, no-time-to-stop lifestyles. Net result – web language was born.

NOT STRICTLY BLACK TIE

Web language is short, less formal and at times quite chatty, but this does not mean to say that the basic rules of grammar and spelling are any less important – it just means that they are slightly more bendy. There is no excuse for mistakes, but if you can be clever with your copy and can imbue your web pages with a bit of humour users will be extremely forgiving (and grateful).

SOUND BYTES

No matter how well crafted each word of text is on any given web page, only a small percentage of them will actually be read. We, the users, will scan quickly,

Here's an
idea for
you...

Choose a random page from your web site – if you have an e-commerce store, choose a product description page. Now rewrite the copy as if you were describing that product to a friend in a bar. Your friend wants to know what is so great about this product and how it is going to improve his life much more than long technical specifications or how good your company or the manufacturer thinks it is. Using this concept, look to re-write the copy across your site. Keep the long, factual descriptions, but put something far more snappy, chatty and friendly as your opening gambit. Your users will appreciate it and just look to your sales for evidence of its effectiveness.

hoping that our eye catches something related to what it is that drove us to this page in the first place. It has to be very well written copy indeed to first gain our attention and second to make us want to change our direction and read more – but it can be done.

Keep your text short, snappy and focused, and make your links obvious. Entice readers by teasing us to read on; writing for the web is all about fighting for users' attention. They will take what they think is on offer and leave, without even a by-your-leave.

Observe your competitors' sites shamelessly. Are they doing something that is different or – admit it, it is possible – something better? If they are funny, make your text funnier. If their site is a little tongue-in-cheek, compete with wit and take the war of words to them.

STOP JABBERING

As a rule of thumb, try not to use more than three paragraphs to describe a product or service. Paraphrasing the old maxim about presentations – tell them what it is, tell them again and remind them what they've just read. Be economical with your words in the first instance. By all means allow users to find out more, such as technical specifications, testimonials, related products, etc., but don't let it get in the way of the synopsis. More often than not, this will be enough to secure the sale, or get the message across, before the user moves on. Users like to know that there is more information available, should they wish, but often just that knowledge often acts as the substitute of actually reading it. The trick is to have information to hand, but for it not to be fighting for space with the sound bite.

Writing excellent copy is only half the battle. The key to good text is good presentation. Check out IDEA 15, *Looking good tonight!*

Try another idea...

'I pray you bear me henceforth from the noise and rumour of the field, where I may think the remnant of my thoughts in peace, and part of this body and my soul with contemplation and devout desires.'
WILLIAM SHAKESPEARE

Defining idea...

'But what is the difference between literature and journalism?...Journalism is unreadable and literature is not read. That is all.'
OSCAR WILDE

Defining idea...

How did it go?

Q **Editorial say that there is no way that we can re-write our entire site, it has taken years to compile. Is there some other way in which we can improve the site?**

A *No one is suggesting that the text you have written is wasted. It's not. It's the factual copy that will give your visitors confidence in you and your products, but they still need to be teased. Just an opening sentence for every product will do the trick.*

Q **Our site is humorous and snappy. Surely we're already there?**

A *Good for you, and you're probably right. But it might be worth getting a friend to try and re-hash a single page of text for you in the style that they think is better. This will either reinforce your confidence or show your house style might have a limited appeal..*

18

Red eye and open mouths

Images are important. They help break up a page of text, they confirm what you are writing about and they can explain things far more succinctly than just words.

Images are absolutely essential on a web site. So wherever possible, use professional images taken and modified through good equipment — leave your old Instamatic safely locked up. Trust me.

IMAGE IS EVERYTHING

Not only is the visual content of your images important, it is essential that you you maximise them for use on the internet. For once, the best is not necessarily the most ideal. Images on a computer monitor can look completely different to the same image printed out on paper. The quality of an image (assuming that it is a good photo or design in the first place) is determined by the pixel size and the number of pixels to be shown per inch (dots per inch, or dpi). When preparing images for printed material, the rule of thumb is to save the image with at least 300 dpi. When you are altering images to be shown on a web site you must turn the dpi down. There is simply no point saving an image at more than 72 dpi because computer monitors can't appreciate the difference. Those companies that insist on higher-resolution images just slow down the load speed of their site. This will annoy users.

Here's an idea for you...

Take a random web page from your site and remove all the text. Leave the images where they normally appear and see if a friend can guess what is going on. The images on the page won't necessarily be self-explanatory, but your friend should have a good idea of what the function of the web page is, just by looking at the images and where they are placed. With the text gone, you'll be able to see with ease how well you are using images across the page. If you find that there are too many close together, or only at the top of the page, you should be looking to address the layout of your web site.

A trick first cornered by large e-commerce stores was to save a small, medium and sometimes even large image of every product on the server. This means that if a customer is just browsing, they can see a thumbnail image of everything in that category or section of the site. If the customer wants to read more about the product, they click on the link and it takes them to the product description page. Here would be the slightly larger image, allowing the customer to scrutinise the product more easily. Lastly, if the customer still wants more, they can click on the image and go to yet another page showing the image at full-page size. And if that doesn't satisfy them, they can buy the product and gaze at it all day long in the comfort of their own home. This tactic helps keep your web site working quickly, but also allows customers to see more of what they want, when they want.

PICTURE THIS

Each web site is unique in terms of what it is trying to achieve and the audience it is trying to appeal to – but all of us are limited by the technology we are using either to host a web site (the server) or view one (the client). Overwhelming your pages with images, unless of course you are an online art gallery, is foolhardy. Either your server or your user's browser will become clogged with sending and receiving information: net result, a slow site and an angry user – neither of which is funny or clever. Choose the images you want to use carefully, ensure that they are maximised for the web and let users choose to see more, if they wish – don't come out with all guns blazing and try to get every image you have on every page. Patience is a virtue (except in slow-loading web sites), and if a consumer chooses to view another image, they are going to spend a lot longer appreciating it that if you force-feed them.

Try complementing your images with effective and eye-catching buttons and links. To find out more, check out IDEA 13, *Smart cookie*.

Try another idea...

IMAGE GUARDIAN

If you want to use an image on your site you must ensure that you have copyright permission to do so. Likewise, it is essential to protect your own images from copyright infringement. There are a number of techniques you can employ – using watermarks, which allow users to view an image but show it belongs to you; only letting people download low-res versions of the image; asking your developers to turn off 'save picture as'. If you have saved the image at 72 dpi, there is nothing really to worry about in terms of printing a copy of the image, because the quality on the printed page will usually be appalling.

'There is nothing worse than a sharp image of a fuzzy concept.'
ANSEL ADAMS

Defining idea...

How did it go?

Q **The design team is concerned that users don't read down to the bottom of the page, so we deliberately design our web pages to be image top heavy. Why should we change?**

A *It isn't essential to change if this works for you. But it might make the web page more attractive if you use a similar, or even the same, image repeated below.*

Q **Our images are always a little bit grainy and not at all pleasing on the eye. What are we doing wrong?**

A *Invest in some photo/image software such as Photoshop. Assuming that you are taking digital images or scanning pictures, you'll be able to doctor the image by changing the resolution and dpi until it looks perfect.*

19

I've got your number

Use your web site to find out who your customers are and what they want. Emails, questionnaires, forms – they're all here.

Be polite, don't beg and don't promise the earth. Make your users want to help you, not be scared of you.

BE COOL, HONEY BUNNY

There is nothing worse than having to register on a web site before you are allowed to proceed to the buy button, or worse, to move on from the homepage. At this stage the user might not have a clue what or who you are, so why on earth are they going to be comfortable giving you their personal details? Even asking for an email address and a password is pretty rude – how do they know if you are going to sell their details on? Net result – the user moves on to another site and is probably gone forever.

If you are a subscription-based service and you want to protect the best information for those who pay – fine, but give your casual users a taster, show them examples, win their hearts and minds and you might get some of their wallet too!

Here's an idea for you...

Next time you are considering launching a new line of products or adding an additional section to your web site, ask your users what they think. A simple (well-written) questionnaire, even without an enticement (such as a gift certificate), will usually result in a 2% response rate. Depending on the number of customers' users' email addresses you are holding, this can be far more productive than your department sitting around a table for a few hours battling it out.

IT'S GOOD TO TALK

No one will trust a web site without a real world contact number or address listed somewhere on the site, and more importantly, we all like to have a moan, make a comment or generally send emails to nameless, faceless corporations around the world. You will receive a lot of nonsense, but it's essential that you create a feedback@yoursite.com email address, so that you can capture and collate user comments.

EVERYTHING IN MODERATION

Limit the number of mailouts you release over any given twelve-month period. Never forget that you are not the only web site that your users visit – each of these web sites will be employing similar tactics, so yours will be one of many unsolicited emails received on that day. Treat your customers as you would wish to be treated yourself (but don't overdo it on the cakes). Be fair, be specific and remember that familiarity breeds contempt.

NO MORE!

Some users won't want to hear a word from you, no matter how great your offers, promotions or 'trusted' third-party organisations might be. These are users who will visit your site on their terms, when they want; and your sending them emails, SMS messages or even calling them on the phone won't endear them to you. These customers are just as important as your other customers, and it's imperative that you offer an opt-out email address for them to write to so that they can't be mailed in the future. Delaying or ignoring this function will lose you their custom quickly, and could get you a bad name.

A PENNY FOR YOUR THOUGHTS

Questionnaires are a great way to get into the mind of your users. Tolerance of long-winded questions is still remarkably high, and I suppose we all like to express our views across the internet. If possible, try to entice people to complete them, it doesn't have to be much –

Maximising forms for effectiveness is never more important than during the order pipeline; turning your visitor from user to consumer is a fine art. Check out more in IDEA 50, *Stick that in your pipe and smoke it!*

Try another idea...

'Quality in a product or service is not what the supplier puts in. It's what the customer gets out and is willing to pay for. A product is not quality because it's hard to make and costs a lot of money, as manufacturers typically believe. This is incompetence. Customers pay only for what is of use to them and gives them value. Nothing else constitutes quality.'
PETER DRUCKER

Defining idea...

consumers will do an awful lot for very little. Try offering a low-value gift certificate, or a three-for-two offer that will mean you get the information you want and an extra sale into the bargain! This will also mean a higher response rate and more honest answers.

NOT ANOTHER FORM!

Forms are an important way to capture user date but they should do so in a non-obtrusive way. There really is nothing worse than spending ten minutes filling out a form on the internet, only to have it spat back at you because you missed out an answer or did not answer it correctly. We all make mistakes (yes, even me), and we should not be punished by a trumped-up web site coming back with a rude message at the top of an otherwise blank screen saying that we are incompetent buffoons who don't even know our own address. Be sure to explain each section well and allow users to fix their errors without having to repeat the entire process.

Q   **Management say we can't ask our customers about a potential new product range as it might give our competitors too much information. Do we run this risk?**

How did it go?

A   *Obviously some things will be business decisions that must be taken at board level, and remain a secret until launch. Instead, ask your users other questions. For example, if you're trying to ascertain how much you can charge for shipping to a certain country, ask only those customers that this will affect and give them three options to choose from. This might confirm what you already know, or it might show that you'll be pricing yourself too high for the market.*

Q   **The customer service team would rather not involve our customers in any marketing mailouts as it might drive them away? Aren't they being a little alarmist?**

A   *Certainly if you start mailing too much, even the most patient of us will start getting angry, but as long as you limit your mailouts, make the unsubscribe function obvious and once in a while throw in a promotion or enticement, consumers will either respond or delete...but if they like everything else about your service, they'll be back.*

20

Getting naked

A site search is a useful option for many a web site, but only if it works properly. You need to think like a user – but what if you're visited by aliens?

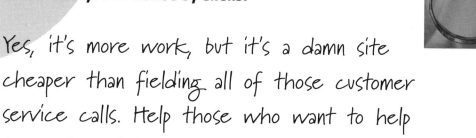

Yes, it's more work, but it's a damn site cheaper than fielding all of those customer service calls. Help those who want to help themselves and keep customer comments to a bare minimum.

A NEEDLE IN A HAYSTACK

When using a reference book, the reader will often use the contents page and index to cross-reference and ensure that they are reading all of the pertinent points. It should be no different for a web site. Although the homepage acts like a table of contents, the sites that let themselves down are those that don't include an index, or site search. By offering a site search you are empowering your user to query your site for the information they want. Although offering this direct route to goal might mean they miss many of the features or offers also available on the site, it's better they get what they came for than leave completely empty handed.

Use your competitors' sites shamelessly to find how well or badly their search facility works. It is only by experiencing frustration yourself that you'll be able to transfer the learning into improving your own offering. Site searches are not functions that work perfectly the moment you switch them on; they need to be tweaked and monitored to ensure that they are still current and returning the information that users need. If you can, capture the words or phrases that visitors are using in your search box. Not only will this show you if your search box is working, it will also give you a good idea of why users are visiting your site, and may help when you are deciding what products or information to include on your homepage.

A BAD SITE SEARCH

A bad site search is when the user must first know what it is they are looking for. It might seem ridiculous that a user is not even sure what information they want, but it happens all the time. The confusion is how they categorise the information and where they think they might find it on your site. If you classify it differently, your perfectly logical buttons and links will seem like random chaos to them. Giving them the option to search, rather than abandon ship, will keep your users happy and give you custom.

A GOOD SITE SEARCH

A good site search asks no questions of the user. Allow them to type in a word and return the results as quickly as possible – listing the most obvious and most popular search results first. Using the example of a music store, don't make them first choose only an artist or only a title, let them search for either or both and bring back the results. When your developers are first creating (or rebuilding) your search function, accept that users will make spelling mistakes, and that some will use punctuation and some will not (especially apostrophes); be sure, as best you can, that what the user searches for need only resemble the correct target. A good web site also allows wildcard searches. This is when a user knows part of a title or a name. For example, if I'm searching for a book that I know has the word *Blood* in the title, I could search for Blood*. This will bring back all of the results containing the word blood, and once I see the search results, my memory is jogged and I know I was looking for *Blood Lust* (each to their own, that's what I say).

Site searches are a great way to let your web site do a lot of the hard work for you. To find out more about using technology to your advantage, check out IDEA 49, *The importance of being lazy.*

Try another idea...

'Basic research is what I am doing when I don't know what I am doing.'
WERNHER VON BRAUN

Defining idea...

'Research is the process of going up alleys to see if they are blind.'
MARSTON BATES

Defining idea...

How did
it go?

Q **Our site is full of data and is not as simple as selling books or CDs. We need a far more detailed search to provide the best service for our customers. How can we get around this problem?**

A *The way round this is to have a general search available throughout the site and to have a separate button offering users the chance to perform a detailed search. A trick is to let users perform a general or quick search; if there are more than ten results, repeat the link to the detailed search at the bottom of the page to allow them to be more specific. But do let the user perform a quick search first – you never know, they might just strike lucky.*

Q **We have monitored the search queries that our customers are performing but they are searching for products or information that is not available on our site. What use is this to us?**

A *This is priceless market information. If enough users think that you might provide them with the answer to their query and you don't already hold those products or that information, it may make sense to change that fact. If that is impossible, look for another web site that does and set up some kind of reciprocal link deal which will be mutually beneficial.*

21
Drop it, now!

Dropdown menus are all about choices and options. Too much of one and not enough of the other is unhealthy. Use sparingly, and only when you need to.

You can never have too much of a good thing — but then, dropdowns are a bad thing if there's no thought behind where they appear on a site.

MORE QUESTIONS THAN ANSWERS

Dropdowns should only really be used when it's imperative that the user is specific – so, when using a currency converter site, it's understandable that we have to choose the currency we are using (e.g. GBP) and the currency we are converting to (e.g. USD). There is no room for error here and the software will only work if these options are used. The same is true for choosing a country for a shipping address, as the result will determine whether the product can be shipped there and the cost of shipping. Dropdowns should not be used when you are offering users a selection of products – this should be solved by clever navigation, browse categories and a search box.

Here's an idea for you...

Look at the areas of your site where dropdowns are currently employed. Is there something that could be done differently to still allow customers the same choice, but not through a menu? Why can't these web page destinations be reached through the site navigation or through the search facility? If your dropdowns are essential, is there anything that you could do to shorten them or make the options more specific? Lastly, imagine that dropdown menus are no longer available; how would you approach replacing your menus and still allow users to navigate the site and make their choices? With the answers to hand, consider implementing the changes in favour of menus – it will make your site slicker, more logical and more user-friendly.

A dropdown is effective when a product is available in different sizes or when you want to limit customers ordering multiple units. In the case of clothing sizes, the dropdown menu will be limited by the sizes you stock, and a good way to control customers from buying too many units of a specific promotion is to only offer a dropdown of numbers (say 1,2,3) rather than allowing them to enter in their own figure.

DON'T BE SMART

Dropdown menus are not the time to start getting witty, ironic or clever with your options. User patience with dropdowns is low at the best of times; what we want when we get there is for the options to be straightforward and obvious. Spell out your menu options in normal English (or whatever the mother language is of the site) and use your creative talents elsewhere. This includes not using confusing words, using slang or shortening words so that the list is more aesthetically pleasing.

DIVIDE AND CONQUER

If your menu ends up too long and becomes unwieldy – sub-divide. There is no point having users scrolling down long lists looking for something specific. Offer categories first and then give the option of a dropdown menu as a last resort.

The only long list that is acceptable, mainly because it has become the industry standard, is the list of countries customers can choose from when subscribing to a site or entering their shipping destination. But there are tricks you can use to make this user-friendly. For one, bring the most common choices to the top of the list and repeat them again in their alphabetical order – so put UK, US to the top of the shipping address dropdown, if the majority of your customers are based there. With the best will in the world, nobody based in Afghanistan is likely to order a product or service from your site, and certainly not in the quantities to justify having their country top of the list. It is pointless to waste the time of your users scrolling through numerous countries before they find their own. Know your users and give them what they want. A personal bugbear of mine is how England is classified in dropdown menus. I don't know whether to search for England, United Kingdom or Great Britain, because depending on the web site it could be any one of them. Put me out of my misery – offer all three options.

**A good way to minimise the need for dropdowns is to improve the search facility on your web site. To find out more, check out IDEA 20, *Getting naked.*

Try another idea...

'It is better to know some of the questions than all of the answers.'
JAMES THURBER

Defining idea...

'Judge of a man by his questions rather than by his answers.'
VOLTAIRE

Defining idea...

How did it go?

Q Our dropdowns work fine, the users get what they want and there have been no complaints. What's the problem?

A *No one is arguing that dropdowns don't work – they do. But sometimes they are not the most effective way of giving users choices and options. If they work fine, that's great, but you should always be looking to improve and enhance your site – both to stay ahead of the competition and to keep your site looking fresh. Run the exercise anyway and try to find a different way to express the options on your dropdown.*

Q We would like to improve our shipping destination dropdown. Do you have any other tips?

A *As well as sorting out Blighty, you might want to look at the countries on the list that your own country currently has trade embargoes with. If you are not allowed to ship to those countries there is no point offering the option. I'd also take a close look at the countries from where you are receiving the most credit card fraud. If the fraud outweighs the trade, it might be worth considering not shipping to those countries at all. Both of these ideas will shorten your country dropdown considerably.*

22

Is that it?

To all intents and purposes, your homepage is your web site – it may be the only link you have to hook your visitors. Get it right and you can dream the dream...

You need to bare all, hide any embarrassment and be proud of how your business looks full frontal on the web...

A LIST IS JUST A LIST?

No. The categorisation of your products or information and how you present it to the user will determine not only how well your site works, but also how well it's received. Creating the perfect homepage is a delicate balance between showing what wonders are contained within the site and not trying to include a little bit of everything, which only leads to confusion. Through clever design, logical links and buttons and not being too outrageous you can achieve this with your homepage. Let users feel that they are searching by themselves, by giving people hints and obvious waypoints without spoon-feeding them.

Here's an idea for you...

Forget about how much it would cost, but imagine that you had the opportunity to re-launch your web site, with an all-new design. What would you do differently, which products or pieces of information would you showcase and what would you leave deeper in the site? How does your homepage differ from those of your competitors and those of unrelated web sites? You're not really comparing style here, just the effectiveness of the homepage to introduce to the visitor what lies within.

GIVE THEM A MAP

Good practice procedures with regard to creating a homepage all boil down to logic. The only flaw is that we all think differently. You must try and get into the mind of your visitor. Although you won't have to do a lot for the web-efficient techie audience out there, they are only a small part of the internet population. Short of a good, old-fashioned Vulcan mindmeld, the next best procedure is all about building and designing to appeal to the techie, whilst actually designing a site for the lowest common denominator. The homepage is where you are laying your cards out on the table, though not necessarily face up. This is a hint of what you have to offer inside. From the homepage, a visitor should be able to go anywhere on the site. If there's no direct link or button (which is understandable on large sites), then there should be the option to search the site, call up help pages, see a site map, browse within categories and generally be wowed by the great copy and images that have the user looking in areas they didn't even know they wanted to visit.

THE BILL OF FARE

What you decide to include on your homepage in terms of text and images and how often these are altered will be determined by the needs of the business. No homepage should ever remain static, no matter what the purpose of the site is. There is nothing worse than reading information on a site that refers to events or products or dates in the future tense when it's obvious that time has moved on. This shows the user that the site is old and not maintained, and it immediately puts into question the validity of anything contained within.

Treat the homepage like the menu at a restaurant (no, not to hide the ketchup bottle): use the space to entice and wet the taste buds, but leave the substance further back within the site. Let your user choose what it is they wish to consume, let the server be the chef and, if your user enjoys what you have to offer, they may even leave a tip.

Getting your message across through a web site is paramount if you want your web site to succeed. There are times and places when it's more advisable to show visitors more or less information. To learn more, check out IDEA 5, *We want information!*

Try another idea...

'In great affairs men show themselves as they wish to be seen; in small things they show themselves as they are.'
NICHOLAS CHAMFORT

Defining idea...

'A man builds a fine house; and now he has a master, and a task for life; he is to furnish, watch, show it, and keep it in repair, the rest of his days.'
RALPH WALDO EMERSON

Defining idea...

How did it go?

Q   We haven't got the facilities to chop and change our web site at will. Although we can alter the soft content (which products are featured etc.), editorial can't alter the hard content (fixed buttons, categories and design) of the site. What else can we do to better present our offering?

A   *That is limiting, especially if even an exploratory meeting with a development house to re-design your site is out of the question financially. Still, it's important to make what changes you can with the tools available to you. If all you are able to alter are the products or paragraphs shown on the homepage, start to employ themes in style. Each week choose four (or however many products you show on your homepage) that are all related in some way. After one week, change the offering. It will quickly become apparent if you are able to view the number of hits and the number of purchases/page views that certain themes or products work better than others. This will also ensure that your site looks fresh and well maintained.*

Q   How can we see what changes work best?

A   *Spend a few weeks altering the positions of buttons on the homepage and the product/s you give precedence to. Collate the information by matching up the visitor numbers with what products were bought or pages viewed. If there's an improvement, consider making the changes more permanent.*

23

Like bad wind

Like cockroaches, pop ups have a role in life. It just isn't very big. So how do you tell a good 'un from a bad 'un?

As with everything, there's a time and a place for pop ups (especially adverts) — preferably when my machine's switched off and I'm asleep. Remember, you might be one pop up away from losing a valued user...

JUST POPPED UP TO SAY HELLO

And probably lost you a customer forever! Pop up windows occasionally appear because the web site owner wants to display information on a separate window for your convenience. A good example of their effective use is when a user is searching through an online help section. This web site regards Help as a separate function to the rest of the site and the user can still view the page that they require assistance with, whilst seeing what they should do next. But the majority of pop ups are advertising windows that hit the user unaware and uninvited, and can quite easily scare the uninitiated.

Here's an idea for you…

If you do currently accept advertising revenue through your web site in the form of pop up adverts, look closely at how much revenue it brings in. You need to be sure that that you are not losing too many users because of it. A great indication of the negative effect of pop up advertising is to compare the number of hits your web site receives with the number of downloads/ purchases/regis-trations or other transactions taking place. This is known as your conversion ratio. If the conversion ratio is lower than normal when there are pop up adverts on your site, then you have a serious problem. You will quickly be able to compare the revenue gained from the adverts with that lost from custom and make the decision to continue accordingly.

Whether you view pornographic sites deliberately or not, this is pop up at its worst. The user lands on a site, wants to leave by clicking back or clicking on the X to kill the screen and – surprise, surprise – numerous windows begin to appear. This tactic is really the lowest of the low and I'd be surprised if it ever works for the advertiser in more than a handful of cases.

HA, HA YOU CAN'T SEE WHAT YOU'RE READING

They are usually the most attractive advertising deals, but pop ups are the surest way to drive traffic away from your site permanently. Pop up technology has and will continue to move on and become ever more advanced. More and more web sites that accept advertising revenue from third-party pop ups are moving away from the basic square window that overrides all other open browser windows and becoming far more subtle. Some pop ups are time delayed and appear to be part of the web site through the clever use of graphics. One minute the user is happily reading through the text on the page and the next minute two characters climb down on ropes from the top of the page carrying with them a banner that covers the information you might be trying to read. This, coupled with the fact that the normal X to kill the screen is sometimes not in the industry standard top right hand corner, means that the user has to at least look at the pop up for enough time to find how to close it down. You may have made some cash from the advertising; but many a customer will give up reading or buying from your site and move on to somewhere else a little more peaceful.

Pop ups are just one of many ways that you can make enemies fast on the internet. You want to create a place that users feel both welcome and safe to visit. For more, check out IDEA 35, *By whatever means necessary.*

Try another idea...

GOOD OUT OF BAD

Some online banks make good use of pop up windows. As an added security precaution – even though the user has passed multiple levels of security to access their personal details, the server only puts up a window containing the specific information requested, such as their statement. By using a pop up window instead of displaying the data in the regular browser window, the bank has more control over the time taken to view the page (automatic logout) and even the functionality of the window, such as turning off the print function. Because it's the user demanding the information, they are more tolerant of pop ups appearing on their screen; but this goodwill will quickly be lost the moment the banks start accepting third-party adverts...

'It shouldn't be too much of a surprise that the internet has evolved into a force strong enough to reflect the greatest hopes and fears of those who use it. After all, it was designed to withstand nuclear war, not just the puny huffs and puffs of politicians and religious fanatics.'
DENISE CARUSO

Defining idea...

105

How did it go?

Q   OK, we've spent some time looking at the pop ups on our site and have realised that they are the only revenue generators on it! Take those out and we've no business left, even if all our visitors are happier than ever. How do we get round that one?

A   *Advertising may be the only route to revenue open to you and that isn't necessarily a bad thing; but pop ups are not the only type of advert you could place on your site. If you discuss with your advertiser your fears about pop ups there may well be other options open to you, such as banner advertising, product placement, mailing lists and sponsored links. Far better to devalue your own site slightly with a fixed or rolling third-party advert than annoy your customers with a pop up.*

Q   We've tried negotiating and pop ups are all that's on offer for the revenue we need. Do we have any choice?

A   *Take the deal if it means your survival but work on creating a sustainable future for your site that does not include pop up adverts.*

24

Don't be shy

Most users are curious to know more about the personalities involved behind a web site. Rogue's gallery, 'My name is Sharon...', email addresses – whatever the method, introduce yourself.

You're not trying to be everyone's best friend, but you need to reveal a bit about your company. Trivia and a few jokes are good; home phone numbers and waist measurements are bad!

WHO ARE YOU?

Don't be shy! Users like to see the personality/ies behind a web site. Whether it be photos of your entire customer services department or you the artist hard at work – the more personal the site, the more users will trust you. It really does make a difference if there are a few photos of the staff somewhere on the site; you would be surprised how many hits these pages receive. Competitors use the pages to size up who they are up against, clients or partners use the pages to see who they are meeting with and hopefully glean a bit of information from the site, and users will visit, mainly out of curiosity, to see what Simon from the warehouse department looks like.

They won't like it. Not one bit. But it's time to add some photos to the web site. And that includes middle and top management. Get some snaps up there; at worst, have everyone bring in a picture of themselves as a child to scan and post onto the site. Even less popular is to focus on a single member of staff, either once a week or once a month. Use a template questionnaire and post the results on the staff area of your site. It can be simple things like favourite holiday destination, book and film but what it does is creates a chink in the wall so that visitors feel more involved with the company they are dealing with.

'The public is wonderfully tolerant. It forgives everything except genius.'
OSCAR WILDE

Let your users into a little bit of your lives and they will reply with hits to your site and purchases.

THE NUMBERS GAME

I recently attempted to find the corporate telephone numbers of the country's leading mobile phone operators regarding a business development proposal. I didn't want their customer services department or recorded messages about new services or opening an account, but these were the only numbers on offer. How dumb does that make these companies look? They make their money out of telecommunications but don't have the wit to list their own number for non-account holders who may wish to talk about something important. Don't be afraid that listing a number will inundate your office with unwanted calls – it won't. But it will allow people to communicate with you in the way they want. Most internet users are comfortable using email/web forms, or customer services when appropriate, but sometimes information is too delicate or time-sensitive to be entered onto a form or sent to your call centre many miles (and maybe continents) away from the corporate HQ, with no way of knowing when it will be read, and by whom. Or whether they will understand it.

CONTACT US – GO ON, PLEASE!

As important as including a telephone number on your web site is for you to include at least one email address that can be used by users to contact you. Whether these mails arrive in a member of staff's mailbox or whether they go into an email queue for your customer services department to answer is irrelevant. Let users contact you with whatever is on their mind. More advanced sites create email addresses for specific queries or comments, which means the question or comment has more chance of arriving at the right place and being answered by the right person. As a minimum, I'd suggest that each site has the following mail addresses set up:

Being transparent is all about giving back to users. Sometimes, in return we can ask for advice and guidance from our visitors in return. For more information, check out IDEA 34, *The importance of being earnest.*

Try another idea...

E-commerce sites
- orders@ or sales@
- returns@
- shipping@
- info@
- contact@
- products@
- technical@
- unsubscribe@

General sites
- info@
- contact@
- unsubscribe@
- editor@ or webmaster@

Posting information about where you are based won't ordinarily result in angry customers knocking on your door. If you write about your location in a positive way it will only increase traffic and custom. People tend to be quite

'Honesty is the best image.'
TOM WILSON

Defining idea...

loyal, either to a city or a country. If you are based in Liverpool, sing about it and show how you are a positive influence on local employment and commerce. Likewise, if you are a Europe-based company and are looking to improve home sales, let your users know you are here (or there, depending on where you are reading this) and show the user how your local knowledge improves your offering.

How did it go?

Q   We sell agricultural machinery; our CEO thinks that a few mug shots are hardly going to improve our sales. How can I convince her otherwise?

A   *You'd be surprised, and it won't cost much to find out – bear in mind that some customers feel there is something lacking with online sales. They like to walk into a physical shop, look around, have a chat with the shopkeeper and make a purchase. By adding some personalities to your site, you are helping to bridge that gap.*

Q   Human resources fear that we run the risk of a member of staff being harassed by a stalker-like customer if we start posting pictures up. Is this not the case?

A   *There are some very weird customers; most of them live in Texas and Iran, if my experience is anything to go by. Certain customers will harass your customer service department whether you post photos and information or not – these people like to chat or moan, it's as simple as that. It is still worth having a go at the exercise anyway. And if the worst comes to the worst, you can always put up a picture of George, the Martin Johnson lookalike from maintenance.*

25

Run away!

Letting go is never easy, I know – but if you want your visitors to return, it's essential. Let them come, let them see and let them go gracefully.

Although they say kidnap victims sometimes begin to empathise with their captors, once they're free they will be the first to testify against you...

DON'T BURN YOUR BRIDGES

Possibly the worst offence in this bracket is to block the back button. Sites employ this tactic to trap visitors. If the user clicks back, the page refreshes and they see the same page again. Ordinarily, a user will click back because they want to go to where they were before. Stopping them from doing it will enrage, not engage.

DON'T POP UP

Likewise, if a user decides to move on to another web site or clicks back, the second worst offence is for one or more pop up screens to attack their vision. For them, something about your site wasn't right, or they have read all they want and it's time

Here's an
idea for
you...

Once a section of your site has been updated or altered in some way, construct about four differently styled emails to let registered users know about it. Break the mailing list into sections and mail out from four separate addresses (mail1@clampcity.com, mail2@clampcity.com etc.). The important thing is to alter the link ever so slightly so that you are able to monitor the web page that is attracting the hits (e.g. www.clampcity.com/promo1). It will take a series of these mailouts before any results become apparent, but over the course of four or five mailouts you should be able to see quite clearly which style of email works best, for which sections of your customer base.

to head off – there's no logic in thinking that they'll be happy to visit a third-party advertiser when they have finished with you.

DON'T I KNOW YOU FROM SOMEWHERE?

Your users won't be as familiar with the layout of your site as you are. Whenever they click on a link on your site, it's important to make sure that the link changes colour. Customers need to scent their trail. Likewise it makes commercial sense to show users whereabouts they are on your site, with a simple text location or graphic at the top of the page. Making visitors repeat themselves will only antagonise. Let them travel at will wherever they may roam throughout your site.

NAME AND NUMBER, SOLDIER

There are sometimes real business needs for making customers log in to your site.

Certainly it is right to encourage users to log in, with the understanding that you can then tailor the site to make it more specific to their needs or reveal confidential information; but don't insist on it until and unless it's absolutely necessary. Let users see as much as possible before making them sign in. This will encourage new users to feel more at home on your site and show your registered users that you take their privacy and trust seriously.

REMEMBER ME?

There are times when you'll need to remind customers that you still exist and you are ready to serve, whether that be products or information. Mailouts are a very effective way to communicate with all of your registered users (assuming they haven't opted out) and in essence 'talk' to them direct about what's new and what's happening at your site. But never forget that you are invading their privacy. You can't just send a mail to say hello, hoping that seeing your web site name again will inspire users to come back – there needs to be a teaser; some attractive lure to bring them back into your manor. Price promotions are a firm favourite, along with time-specific offers. For information-based sites you can tell your users about updated pages on the site, or new sections they may not have seen before. Try to do your homework, though, and limit the mail to only those who you are confident will be interested.

Letting your users come and go as they please and attracting them back when the time comes is all about building a healthy relationship with your users and the formation of your web site as a community-based site. To learn more, check out IDEA 46, *There's no place like home.*

Try another idea...

'Before he sets out, the traveler must possess fixed interests and facilities to be served by travel.'
GEORGE SANTAYANA

Defining idea...

'Remember that happiness is a way of travel – not a destination.'
ROY M. GOODMAN

Defining idea...

113

How did
it go?

Q **Our marketing manager really only wants to be mailing our customer base about twice a year max. It's going to take ages to find out what style works best. Is this the best policy?**

A *That is a great policy and will be appreciated by your customers. The trick is to alter your mailout style drastically if you feel it's not working as well as it should (<2% response rate). Have someone else construct the email, with only the hard facts to work with. Even if you feel it's not your style, assuming that it's grammatically correct and is in keeping with your house style (albeit tenuously), go with it and see what happens.*

Q **But with only two mailouts per year, it'll be a long time before we have it perfected. How can we speed up matters?**

A *Start splitting your customers into groups. Choose one group of customers to receive mailout 1 and another group to receive mailout 2. This way, although each customer is only receiving two mails per year, you are testing numerous writing styles.*

26

Breast implants

Don't be shy about what you have to offer to visitors. Be proud, be daring and give them a bit of metaphorical cleavage to whet their appetites.

Imagine you are dressing a nice but dim man/woman up for an evening on the town. Emphasise all that is good and tell them to keep their mouth shut.

UP AND TO THE FRONT

No matter how much or little content you have within your web site, the key to using space effectively is to push it up and to the front. The simple rule is to push the most appealing or important products or articles to the top of the page, with everything else forming a frame. These words, images or products are your best assets – your family jewels – and must be promoted and supported accordingly. Bearing in mind that many users won't scroll to the bottom of the page, ever, what is above the fold (and therefore will be seen the most) must entice, tease and fulfil your visitor's curiosity enough to read on.

Having said this, under no circumstances leave users who do venture to the nether regions of the page completely stranded. Give them a way to move on, through

Here's an idea for you...

Try to convince the other product managers or content providers responsible for your site to remove half of the images, text, sections, links and references on your homepage for one week only. All of these articles or products will still be available through the various buttons and links – but the actual homepage will be showcasing a fraction of what it used to. Your conversion ratio (the number of users reading the information or buying products) will rise and you won't see a huge drop in the sales or consumption of other areas of the site.

If this works in principle, look to adopt the theory across the web site. The text that you remove need not be wasted; it can placed in new sections of the site that will still be read by users so long as you show them where to find it.

links that replicate the buttons at the top of the page, without making them scroll all the way back up to the top. Let them move on, and sharpish.

GIVE ME THE FULL HIT

Let users click on the image to see a bigger version – don't hit them with large images in the first instance. Tease with a thumbnail image and a little bit of text. If that gets their mouse salivating, then they'll click to find out more. If thumbnails are unsuitable, provide a medium-sized image to begin with (about 144 × 200 pixels) and let them click again to see it in all its glory – any more will be too slow to load and will negate the impact of the larger image, because the user will get bored waiting – especially if there are several images on the page.

When you do offer buttons, images or links on a page, ensure that the name of the destination page is exactly the same as the button or link used to get there. If Fred clicks on a link to read more about Korean Heating Systems, make sure the page he arrives at is titled Korean Heating Systems (not Korean Eating Systems).

TOO MANY COOKS...

Busy sites do not inspire the visitor to make an effort to read or look at what is on offer. The old maxim of less is more once again comes into play in terms of positioning your text, images, buttons and links. This will make the page top heavy and might leave your bottom a tad underdressed. But don't worry – you can use that space effectively to showcase second level products/promotions/information using good text and good images.

JUST LIKE A FILING CABINET

Tabs are a great way to visually show what you have on offer and let your users choose what areas of the site they are interested in viewing. By running the categories of your web site along the top of the page you are saving valuable real estate on the rest of the page for even more buttons or showcasing of products. This is a convention that was pioneered and championed by Amazon and has now become the industry standard. The trick is to ask your developers to use as few images as possible. Text based is best, but if you are determined to use images, keep them simple. Ensure that your tabs are colour coded and it's obvious to the user which category or product range they are currently within. To show that your buttons are in fact tabs, it makes sense to automatically select a tab when users first log on to your site – this can either be a generic welcome page or the most popular product range.

Using space effectively starts with what you offer visitors on your homepage – to make sure your message is understood check out IDEA 15, *Looking good tonight!*

Try another idea...

'Noise is the most impertinent of all forms of interruption. It is not only an interruption, but is also a disruption of thought.'
ARTHUR SCHOPENHAUER

Defining idea...

'If confusion is the first step to knowledge, I must be a genius.'
LARRY LEISSNER

Defining idea...

How did
it go?

**Q   The buyers say that there is simply too much on our site to leave
out. It must all be represented on the homepage. How can I argue
against that?**

A   *Refuse. It's back to too much noise. You will only be diluting your own
offering if you try to cram it all in onto the homepage. Certainly give users
the option of travelling around the site through navigation options, but use
space effectively and don't try to cram.*

**Q   How do we go about choosing which links and images to leave in
and which to temporarily remove?**

A   *First choose those links, products and images which have led to positive
sales in the past. If that doesn't work, you can always run the exercise
again with another set of products.*

27

Laid bare

You're lost. You're panicking. The last thing you feel like doing is spending money. You just want to get out of here! Perhaps I should have a site map...

Remember that a site map is yet another way you can show your full offering off — that, and they're quite good fun to draw...

DO NOT PASS GO

Good web design is all about letting users go where they want. We all think differently, and what is a very logical site to you might be completely wacky to your user – so be transparent and show that your site does indeed have limitations (in terms of the finite number of categories or areas available).

Many webmasters argue that including a site map allows users to bypass their well thought out navigation paths, and therefore users aren't subjected to the full, all-powerful 'magic' of the site. Absolute rubbish. If your visitor can't find, in a very limited amount of time, what it is they want, then they're going to up sticks and leave – and probably for good. By offering them a site map, yes, they might miss out of great offers, witty copy and stunning images – but they'll get to where they wanted to go. Surely that is much more important, and, if their first visit was

Here's an idea for you... **If you don't already have a site map, this should be addressed – no matter how small your site. Even if you your site is a DIY. job using the latest glitzy software, a map can be created automatically by the program and added as a page. If developers have created your site, ask them to map it out. This should not be expensive, as they should already have created the necessary information when they built the site in the first place. If you already have a site map featured on your site, make sure that all the locations are clickable and direct the user to that page.**

deemed to be a success, they are far more likely to return in the future. They might still partake in your promotions and appreciate your huge range, just not right now. Be patient, dear child.

HELP! I NEED SOMEBODY

You can never reinforce things too many times on a web site and therefore it's a shrewd manoeuvre indeed to include the site map as part of your Help page, even if it has its own link or button on the homepage. Users do not think alike (that's how you tell they're not fools), and while some will spot the direct reference, others will assume that you have hidden it within the Help pages – either way, if your site map is sited (and cited) on multiple pages, it will be sighted – simple as that. You've been through the trouble of creating it – so go on, show it off as many times as you can.

CLICK FOR DESTINATION

Make sure that if you go to the trouble of creating a site map, users can interact with it. There is nothing more frustrating for a user than finding a beautifully presented site map, with funky arrows and a London Underground-esque layout, that you are supposed to commit to memory. The pages or areas that you highlight on the site map must be clickable – don't expect users to be able remember and try to travel through your convoluted site structure from memory alone. If I can find what I am looking for on your map, I want to be able to go to that very page immediately; if not, I want out!

I DIDN'T KNOW THAT!

Not only is a site map a cheap and easy navigation tool for visitors, it also gives you the opportunity to show them all of the other sections that they may not have been aware of! It's a backdoor way to promote all the secrets of your web site. They might have first come to your site looking for information about their favourite recording artistes, but notice that you are also a finance provider and actually end their session by signing up for a loan as well as buying a few CDs.

With web sites, logical does not always mean obvious; you need to coax and influence your users and spell things out. For more about clear web sites check out IDEA 14, *As clear as mud*.

Try another idea...

'Maps encourage boldness. They're like cryptic love letters. They make anything seem possible.'
MARK JENKINS, writer

Defining idea...

'Even with the best of maps and instruments, we can never fully chart our journeys.'
GAIL POOL, writer and critic

Defining idea...

How did it go?

Q Our site consists of only a handful of pages; the developers are suggesting that a site map might be overkill. Are they correct?

A *No, it shows that you are a user-friendly web site, and although you might think that the five pages are easy to navigate, your users may have a different opinion. They don't have to use the site map, but it's there if they want to.*

Q Our site is enormous; it's impossible to map each page as they are dynamically created depending on what the visitor wants to view. The IT Director says that a map is simply not possible. I'm sure he knows what he's talking about – doesn't he?

A *When dealing with dynamic web pages, you don't need to map out every product or article – you should be looking to list the categories or topics covered by the site, even if this is covered by the buttons and links available elsewhere. What a site map should be doing is offering your users yet another way to reach the area they want to go, not the only way.*

28

Big planet, little planet

When creating or reworking your web site, it's important to remember that the internet is a global phenomenon. Be prepared for different currencies, different languages and different challenges.

Be aware that you're attracting a global audience, with a variety of views, politics and expectations. Just who is looking at your site and what do they carry in their wallet?

WHO INVITED YOU?

Remember, it won't just be users from your own country hitting your site. If you're selling products, then this is usually not an issue; in fact, a global audience is precisely what you want. Your pricing and shipping options will quickly dictate whether your foreign visitor will stay or go. But when your web site includes views, statements, opinions, news or anything else that can possibly offend, then unfortunately someone, somewhere will probably get upset. This can't be avoided and should not be a reason to hold back on posting your information – after all, where would we be if free expression were not allowed? (Answers on a picture postcard, please.) But there can be a fine line between witty, playful content and

If you are unwilling or unable to offer multi-currency transactions on your web site, a cheaper alternative, for similar benefit, is to offer a currency conversion next to each product or within the shopping basket feature of the site. This can either be hard-coded into the web site or you could offer a link to a third-party conversion site. Although the price quoted to the customer won't be the _de facto_ price that they are charged, it will be very close.

upsetting the entire Christian (or Muslim, or Jewish, or vegetarian) community. By all means post, but be mindful that individuals and organisations, no matter how obscure, can access your site and may decide to launch a vindictive attack – be it a court case, naming and shaming, or encouraging bad publicity for you or your organisation. It's a big world, but at times it can seem very small...

EXCHANGE RATE MECHANISM

A quick win for your site, to help encourage international customers, is to offer multi-currency payments. In relative terms, compared with the charges you'll be paying already to accept transactions in your own currency, setting up and implementing multi-currency transactions are not that much more expensive. As consumers ourselves we often see the price of a product in dollars or sterling and convert it back to, say, euros, but this can be tedious and inaccurate. The beauty of offering multi-currency transactions is that the user can see immediately what the actual charge to them will be, in a currency that they are familiar with. This will inspire confidence in your site from foreign users and can also give the impression that you are a much larger organisation than you really are.

Defining idea...

'Finance is the art of passing currency from hand to hand until it finally disappears.'
ROBERT W. SARNOFF

WHAT'S THAT IN ENGLISH?

It is important to understand the shifting value of currencies around the world and how this impacts on customers and the value of transactions. If you are a UK-based internet retailer, a weak pound will bring you more customers and on paper this looks great. However, if you only accept payments in sterling, by the time the bank has converted the money you'll be left with a lot less than you'd hoped for. Likewise, a strong pound will also impact on your overseas sales, by putting buyers off. Put simply, the same product is costing your foreign customers more than it did before, even though you may have even dropped your sterling price. Your international sales will probably fall as a result. By offering multi-currency payment options you won't magically bypass the whole-world-of-pain that is the exchange rate – but you'll be giving consumers confidence in the prices you offer on your site, in a language and currency that they understand. You will remain expensive to some and cheap (and let's hope cheerful) to others, but you will be less likely to lose sales because of user fear about the real cost by offering them that information.

Letting users know what your site has to offer in the clearest possible way is half the battle with regard to keeping visitors happy. For more information, check out IDEA 31, *Time please, gentlemen.*

Try another idea...

'When I am asked, "What do you think of our audience?" I answer, "I know two kinds of audiences only – one coughing, and one not coughing".'
ARTHUR SCHNABEL

Defining idea...

'Condense some daily experience into a glowing symbol, and an audience is electrified.'
RALPH WALDO EMERSON

Defining idea...

127

How did
it go?

Q **The marketing department is keen, but the finance department fears that offering multi-currency will increase our risk to fraudulent payments. Are they right to be cautious?**

A   *Sadly, fraud is always going to occur, regardless of the currencies you offer on your site. Accepting currencies other than your own will only increase the transactions taking place on your site; it will not lead to a higher level of fraud, as you'll still have the same security features in place (or through a third party) to check the payment card, whether payment is in sterling or another currency.*

Q **The guys in finance are concerned that it will take longer for us to receive our money from consumers. Is this the case?**

A   *Not at all. The customer's card is still being charged when you ship the product and the money will transfer into your account as per usual.*

29

Shout and say your words slowly

We are very lucky that English is often regarded as the language of the net and commerce. By ignoring other languages, you are blocking potential users from interacting with your site.

It's time to dust off those high school textbooks and get down with the lingo — mine's a cafe solo por favor...

SPEAKING IN TONGUES

Non-English-language versions of your web site are not created overnight, nor will the cost of translation be cheap. Taking the step to offer a multi-lingual site is something that must be thought over in depth, involve all functions of the business and be budgeted for. The overriding question must be: Will a multi-lingual version of our web site add value for customers and for us? If the answer is no, save yourself the project management nightmare and spend the money taking a busman's holiday to these far-off climes instead.

Make a business case for your site to be translated into two additional languages. What would be the benefits to the company, which two languages would be best and what competition are you facing from web sites written in those languages and operating in those countries? The plan may well show that making your site multi-lingual is not a viable option. However, it could reveal a huge opportunity that can be easily exploited.

FLYING THE FLAG

If you decide you need, or have already implemented, a multi-lingual site, well done! Multi-lingual sites are difficult projects to manage and maintain, but the benefits if they are done right can be immense. Deciding to launch a multi-lingual site is a massive step, and not a decision to be taken lightly. Every single word needs to be represented in each of the languages you have on your site. This makes editing information or adding new information both time-consuming and costly.

Defining idea...

'If the English language made any sense, a catastrophe would be an apostrophe with fur.'
DOUG LARSON

The margins for error are enormous and it's only when an error is brought to your attention by a user (unless a member of staff is fluent in each of the languages) that you know to make an alteration – and how many hundreds or thousands of visitors saw the mistake? On the positive side, quite simply you are making your site much more accessible and this will win you points with foreign visitors. If you are offering multi-lingual versions of your site, shout it from the rooftops, and while you're there, plant the flags of the languages in a prominent position at the top of the page.

Managing content and organising specific days when changes to the site are made are never more important than when you offer information in a variety of languages. To learn more about how to minimise errors on your site and keeping a fresh appearance, check out IDEA 42, *Chained to the kitchen sink.*

Try another idea...

'*Language exerts hidden power, like a moon on the tides.*'
RITA MAE BROWN

Defining idea...

'*Think like a wise man but communicate in the language of the people.*'
WILLIAM BUTLER YEATS

Defining idea...

How did it go?

Q **Our IT people have offered to test a multi-lingual version of the site by translating the content through a web-based software translator. Will this have the desired effect?**

A *Absolutely not! The English language, some argue, is the most confusing in the world and no software can match the ability of a live human translator when it comes to translating web site content. It may be expensive, but a translation must be done properly. If your translation is riddled with errors it will be embarrassing and will alienate users. Do it properly or not at all.*

Q **The marketing department argues that we would be better to launch specific sites in those countries rather than confusing the UK site with four different languages. It would certainly be easier to organise, but is it the right thing to do?**

A *Three separate international sites on top of your own is going to get expensive, whether you physically staff the site offices abroad or not. It would be much cheaper to buy the foreign domains (.es .it .fr etc.) and make your main site multi-lingual. If a user clicks on the .co.uk site it will default to English, but they can choose to read in Spanish, and vice versa if they visit the .es site.*

30

It's your fault!

Your web site will sometimes develop faults. With web site management, you must acknowledge that mistakes do happen, and learn to fix them as quickly as possible.

To err is human, but to blame others is lower than the belly of a snake, so the old Chinese proverb states. But hey, it's natural — and it's not my fault!

THE BLAME CULTURE

The network people will blame the software engineers who will blame the designers who will blame the user...That's all very well, but meanwhile there are numerous users unable to view your entire site, or there is a single user trying to locate a page that is no longer available. Both scenarios are equally important – your web site is not delivering, and given that you seldom get a second chance, this error is losing your web site visitors and trade.

If you don't have a branded error page, be sure to have one created. Although this will only catch some user errors (or users trying to visit old removed pages), it all helps establish your relationship with your users as one of good communication. Now, open your internet browser and type your own domain name as fast as you can. Because of habit you are likely to get it right, but repeat the exercise until you don't and write down what you typed by mistake. Look to buy the domain names with this spelling and have the page redirect to your main page – you'll capture a surprising number of extra visitors through this tactic – for very little outlay.

'To err is human, but to really foul things up requires a computer.'
Farmers' Almanac, 1978

PAGE UNAVAILABLE...

Arghhhh! There is nothing worse (other than stubbing your toe and snapping off the nail) than visiting a web page stored in your favourites and the screen telling you that the page is unavailable. Except, perhaps, when a company mounts a marketing campaign and directs users to a specific page that doesn't exist or work. Why bother with the marketing campaign in the first place? Better to give the money to charity, or towards an ad for a new developer. But sometimes (well actually, a lot of the time) it's user error, and whilst you'll never truly know how badly users spell or how a URL (Universal Resource Locator – a web address) longer than two letters is hard work for some visitors, you could do a little more to acknowledge their mistakes and keep them contained within the site.

GIVE ME A SIGN

Often, when users mistype a URL or are pointed to a page that no longer exists, they receive a generic browser error page that gives them no idea of what went wrong. Now the determined visitor will simply click on their back button and try something else, but many will just go and visit another site. Another customer lost. Offer your users a branded error page, not a standard browser window error page, when they (or your site) make a mistake. Keep it simple, but keep them feeling safe:

- You seem to be searching for a page that no longer exists on our web site. Click here to return to the homepage.

- Keep the user connected to your server, don't let them get confused, and give them some indication that you know there is something wrong here (even if it's their mistake).

Minimising errors on the site is a great way to keep your visitors content. For other tricks of the trade, check out IDEA 47, News from the front.

Try another idea…

'The most overlooked advantage to owning a computer is that if they foul up there's no law against whacking them around a little.'
JOE MARTIN

Defining idea…

THINKING DOWN AS WELL AS UP

Minimising site error is possible through good planning and logical mapping on your site. Think through your site design right down to the bottom level; don't think that by organising your homepage, first and second level pages (say, up to the product detail page) that the hard work stops there and that the other pages will automatically make sense. If the page is available, then it's going to be viewed. Just as we judge restaurants and bars on the state of their toilets, so users will be left with an unpleasant smell if a link doesn't take them to where they wanted to go, causes an error page or brings them to a part of the site which is not in keeping (stylewise) with where they have just come from.

'The most likely way for the world to be destroyed, most experts agree, is by accident. That's where we come in; we're computer professionals. We cause accidents.'
NATHANIEL BORENSTEIN

Defining idea…

135

**Q There are numerous spellings of our web site domain name. We'd
have to buy hundreds. Management have stated quite clearly that
it's a waste of money. What can we do?**

*A You don't have to buy every combination of letters – look to see what the
common mistakes are. Get five people who aren't familiar with your
company to type your domain name three times in quick succession. This
should highlight the common errors.*

**Q The hosts of our web site are planning an outage for four hours in
one week's time. What do we do?**

*A Add a small message to your homepage immediately informing users of this
planned outage in advance – the more people who see the message, the
fewer who'll be surprised when the time comes and there is no site there.*

31

Time please, gentlemen

Treat others as you would like to be treated yourself and you're onto a winner. A polite web site is a good web site, and a pleasure to visit time and again.

Let your users know how much they mean to you, but never make it obvious that you are begging for business (even if you are) — that would be silly.

WHAT'S THE TIME, MR WOLF?

A simple trick, but one that will subconsciously show that your web site is both fresh and current is to include the date and even the time somewhere on the homepage (usually near the top). Most users will have a clock showing on their toolbar, but it doesn't hurt to show them again, and remember, not all of your visitors are based in the same country or time zone as you – if you are offering customer service assistance between certain hours, it's nice to let users know if they can contact you right now.

Here's an idea for you... **Assuming that you already have your email/web page blurbs written and you already send polite notes to your users to let them know what's going on, subscribe to/order from a few rival sites or information-based sites (such as online news providers) and look closely at how well they inform their clients. Can anything be learnt from their communications? At worst (or at best, if it's a rival), this will show you, quite clearly, how not to do it!**

Showing the date, especially if you run an e-commerce web site, is an inspired move because it can cause impulsive sales. Users may only be browsing, but reminding them of the date might jog their memory regarding a birthday or an anniversary. They may have had no intention of buying when they hit your site, but now you've reminded them about little Johnnie's birthday, he could be in for a treat – and so could you.

DON'T MIND ME, I'M ONLY THE CUSTOMER

Without users, all web sites are pretty useless (and some are pretty useless anyway). We post information or products on to a web site for others to consume. It is staggering how many web sites take their consumers for granted. If a customer enters a high street store and uses a payment card for a purchase, they can see the clerk swiping the card and the receipt being printed, and then they sign or enter their PIN number. Buying is interactive and physically involves both the seller and the buyer. Online purchases, within reason, should be no different. Your site will request the customer's card details and then call up the bank or a clearing house to authorise the sale; show this process visually. If your server is consulting a bank, let the customer know; even a simple sand timer is better than an apparently crashed site.

Communication should not stop with the taking of money. You may be itching to run off and count your takings, but the customer is now looking for email confirmation that the order has been received and sometime soon, depending on your product and supply chain, will be expecting confirmation that the goods have been despatched. Both functions are simple enough to install and, as well as being incredibly informative, are incredibly polite. And you could just generate repeat sales.

KNOWLEDGE CAN BE BOUGHT

Subscription-based web sites should offer their users an even greater level of communication, given that users are paying to visit and consume information or product. Let your subscribers know well in advance about any alterations to the web site, the terms of their subscription, their level of access or, most importantly, if there will be any server downtime. If downtime is necessary to update servers or for maintenance, make your communication upbeat; explain that 'the downtime is necessary to improve our service to you'. Focus on the positive results post-fix and give subscribers lots of advanced warning.

Letting your users know the date and time is your way of helping them, but communication can be two-way. To learn more about tapping into the views and thoughts of your users, and using it to your advantage, check out IDEA 34, *The importance of being earnest.*

Try another idea...

'Everybody gets so much information all day long that they lose their common sense.'
GERTRUDE STEIN

Defining idea...

Where is the wisdom we have lost in knowledge?
Where is the knowledge we have lost in information?
T. S. ELIOT

Defining idea...

How did it go?

Q **The marketing department is very reluctant to announce planned site downtime because it will alert our rivals to the failings of our network and infrastructure. Surely it's better to timetable the downtime in the middle of the night and say nothing – then no one will be any the wiser. Is this not the way of damage limitation?**

A *First, not all your users are based in the same country as you, so the time of the downtime is not so important, although it is wise to minimise the impact. Secondly, by rebooting servers in the middle of the night, you'll be paying more for your staff's time and it will leave them tired and less effective the next day.*

Q **Surely it still makes sense to keep quiet about downtime though?**

A *Sometimes it can go wrong and one-hour downtime quickly becomes four hours. If you announce in advance that there may be some disruption to your usual service users will feel informed and be less disappointed if it all doesn't quite go to plan.*

32

Smart, dynamic, G.S.O.H. and washes regularly

Are you happy standing still and letting users poke around you or would you rather get up and interact with them? With dynamic web pages, you can.

Don't be frightened of databases — they're not big and scary (anymore), they won't hurt you and they're not too expensive. However, database administrators are a completely different story...

ARE YOU DYNAMIC?

You might think you are, but unless there is a database or two feeding information to your web server, the chances are your web site is static HTML. In principle there is nothing inherently wrong with static web pages, in the same way that there is nothing wrong with exposing yourself in public, but both will leave an unflattering image in the mind of the unsuspecting viewer.

Although alterations and improvements should never be made just to keep up with the Joneses, technology has and does move on, at a staggering rate, and your users will judge the quality of your site quite simply by how it looks and performs. In this

Here's an idea for you...

If you run a static web site, start looking at quotes for a dynamic database-driven web site. Put the argument forward, to those responsible for setting the budget, that a dynamic site is the best way to progress. If you are already database-driven, look at adding additional features that will add to the community aspect of the site, such as a message board or a guestbook.

high-tech world in which we all live, everyone is looking for the site that will put its head above the parapet, but they'll happily shoot it down if it continues to code in HTML 2.0. Users expect, if not demand, change and progress. Using a database to drive your site will help.

WHAT'S IT ALL ABOUT?

Dynamic web sites are primarily those sites that offer categories of products or information and allow users to browse, search or interact online. No matter what choice the user makes, the database will throw up the nearest match/es and hopefully the user will be happy with the results. A dynamic web site is far more versatile than a static one, and ordinarily, new products or new information can be added very easily, often through an interface, which means that non-technical staff can help 'build' the site without fear of getting it horribly wrong and causing widespread damage – again!

CHEAP? NO, NOT REALLY

A dynamic web site will come at a premium. Although the cost of web site design and building has come down significantly over the years, a dynamic web site is more difficult to create and maintain and therefore will cost more. But don't let the

Defining idea...

'Strong lives are motivated by dynamic purposes.'
KENNETH HILDEBRAND

144

additional cost prevent you from offering your users the best that you can. Go on, raise the stakes – be exciting and dynamic if you dare!

WHERE'S YOUR TOOL?

Creating a dynamic web site or more accurately, adding dynamic features to your existing web site all adds to the stickiness of your site – the ability to keep users there, thinking about you or your services and making them much more likely to consume and tell their friends. For some quick wins, and depending on what will suit your site and your offering, look to add interactivity. This can be in the form of a guest book, community message board, weblog or alternating products on the homepage, which can be activated either on a rotation basis or, for the super-slick, dependent on what your user has bought or viewed in the past. Making your users feel at home is more likely to make them want to put the kettle on and their feet up on the table…

Offering dynamic pages and functionality is one way to keep users coming back to your site again and again. To learn more about attracting repeat business, check out IDEA 52, Sticky buns.

Try another idea…

'That which is static and repetitive is boring. That which is dynamic and random is confusing. In between lies art.'
JOHN A. LOCKE

Defining idea…

'Change is the constant, the signal for rebirth, the egg of the phoenix.'
CHRISTINA BALDWIN

Defining idea…

How did it go?

Q   I managed to get the quotes and put the argument forward, but as our site is not product-based, my boss wasn't at all convinced. What else could I say to tip the balance?

A   *Look to use the database as a way to manage all of your customer or subscriber details. The web site might work fine without the services of a database server fetching information, but imagine what you could do with the customer details that you have captured over the years.*

Q   Sorry, I'm being thick here. What exactly would that allow us to do that we can't do already?

A   *By capturing user details in a database you can pull off stats and information almost at will. Depending on how deep you want to mine the data, you'll be able to pull up details on past purchases, average order value, location of buyers and time of purchases, to name but a few. Absolutely invaluable for future advertising campaigns and for truly understanding your business.*

33

You at the back, stop copying

If you put something onto the internet, someone will download it. Which is nice. Just so long as you control the terms and conditions – and keep your jewellery in a box.

Gone are the days when the internet promoted free sharing of information. Free dinners are now off the menu — so charge what you can for every serving, even the cold chips.

SHOW ME WHAT YOU GOT

It is important that your web site provides information of some description and that this information can be accessed by users; after all, that is the point of the World Wide Web...But in this cut-throat commercial world the author/provider of the content must be acknowledged and rewarded – whether that be in fiscal terms or just in copyright acknowledgement.

Although the founding principle was that all information posted on the internet should be available for free, it wasn't long before organisations wised up to the fact that information that is in demand can come at a charge. What is at stake here is

Here's an idea for you...
Look at the viability of protecting all of the images on your web site (assuming that you are the copyright holder); this can be done quickly and cheaply by reducing the file size. If your images are particularly rare/special/unique you should talk to a developer about using watermarks or turning off the browser's 'save image as' function. For text-based documents of importance or value, you should look to remove this text from the source code and make it available instead through a download, such as a PDF file.

the ability to offer information, and as many organisations themselves have to pay for the creation of content, they must pass this cost on (hopefully for profit) to the end-user. And this is where we enter the murky waters of public domain. No matter what protection you may think copyright offers you, unless your developers actually turn the functionality off, every word, image, product, price and typo can be lifted quite easily from your web site and used elsewhere, without the copyright owner being paid and most likely without them even knowing...

LAP-DANCE RULES

That's where PDF (Portable Document Format) comes into play. By saving and posting a file as a PDF, you can answer the need to provide information but protect that information by allowing viewers to see, but not touch. PDFs are marvellous in that large documents can be attached to a web site in the form of a download, available to anyone who requires them; but the content of the document can't be directly altered or stolen. Web site and copyright owners are happy and the end-user is happy.

Defining idea...
'Art does not reproduce the visible; rather, it makes visible.'
PAUL KLEE

SIGN YOUR NAME ACROSS MY HEART

Images can also be protected by a number of methods. First, by setting the resolution to 72 dpi (dots per inch) you'll maximise the quality of the image as viewed on a web site, but it will look dreadful should somebody print it out. Secondly, by saving the image as a small .gif or .jpeg, users will be able to look at and even steal the image but will not be unable to make it any bigger without the image quality suffering. Finally, you can use watermarks to protect your images. Many image sites mark every one of their images with a shadowy name across the image, which brands it as their own. When viewed on the host web site, this image looks clean and respectable and is clearly the property of someone; when 'borrowed', the image appears to be exactly what it is: stolen property!

Try another idea...

Allowing users to view or download files or PDFs from your web site adds significant value to your offering. This can be complemented by offering music, recorded interviews or digital film. To learn more about using moving images and sound files within a web site, check out IDEA 51, *The sound and the celluloid.*

Defining idea...

'Neither a borrower nor a lender be; For loan oft loses both itself and friend; And borrowing dulls the edge of husbandry [economy].'
WILLIAM SHAKESPEARE

Defining idea...

'It is a poor wit who lives by borrowing the words, decisions, inventions and actions of others.'
JOHANN KASPAR LAVATER

149

How did
it go?

Q   How do we go about turning a document into a PDF?

A   You will need to purchase Adobe Acrobat. Once installed, you can print to Acrobat Distiller much like you would to a regular printer. Instead of getting a paper print out, Distiller will create a PDF copy of your document which can be sent as an attachment or posted onto your web site.

Q   Our photographer is not that precious about his images. He's not too concerned about copyright infringement. We'd rather not involve ourselves in the whole messy business. Could this prove problematic in years to come?

A   If he isn't, you should be. Allowing users to steal your images is foolish and you are cutting off a potential revenue stream. If you have great images, someone, somewhere will want them too – and will be willing to pay for the privilege. Charge them, albeit a small fee.

34

The importance of being earnest

The best people to comment on how well your site works are those who use it. So ask them. Abuse, praise, questions and obscure comments are all valuable feedback.

Annoying, needy and very time consuming — but we desperately need them and their money. So take a deep breath, adjust your fig leaf and start proactively interacting with your customers...

PROCESS THIS

For many e-commerce sites, the most common email communications from customers refer to orders not yet received, delayed or lost in the post, or the wrong item being received. Assuming that you have dealt with the customer's issue, you are now left with lots of information that should be captured. Log the number of delayed or lost shipments and show the report to your courier. Ideally they will

Here's an idea for you...

Create a questionnaire to gauge users' opinion of your homepage. As this is probably the showpiece of the web site, it's a good place to start. Your questions should focus not on the aesthetics such as colours (although one question of this ilk is fine) but on the functionality and ease-of-use of the page. Include space for users to include their own comments and leave them with to finish the statement: If I could change one thing on the homepage it would be...

The answers will be varied and strange, but you'll probably end up with a good number of alterations that need to be made to the homepage. These answers are coming straight from your users. Their reactions are real, if sometimes odd and medication-driven, and will help give you an insight into who uses your site and why.

agree to compensate you for your loss. Or, the information will spur you into finding a replacement courier, and you'll immediately have a benchmark against which to measure them. If there are numerous items being sent to the wrong addresses, then you have an issue with your supply chain; either this is a software error and the wrong items are being assigned to the wrong customer despatch note, or, more likely, it's human error and better checks need to be in place in the warehouse. Monitor complaints about slow customer service – it could be that the user is expecting the impossible, and there really is nothing that can be done to improve response times. However, the chances are that improvements can be made and, by monitoring patterns of complaints, you'll be in a much better position to deal with the situation. So, although receiving a barrage of complaints from customers does mean a lot of work, by paying attention to the big picture you'll be able to minimise the same mistakes happening again in the future.

SILVER LINING

When it comes to airing views, customers are often as happy to give positive feedback as negative comments. The trick is devising a system that will coax the information out of them. But before you can start mailing your customers, you need to decide what to ask them. When approaching customers for feedback, be as specific as possible. Asking users whether they like your site will result in some very bizarre answers, and although you may be happy that Mrs Dwyer thinks the yellow background is wonderful because it's the same colour as her canary, you have only succeeded in wasting everybody's time. Be clear about what you are assessing – how satisfied are you with the choice available on our site? How satisfied are you with our delivery charges? Etc. Allow users to mark you out of 5 and allow for extra comments at the end of the questionnaire. Try not to ask more than seven questions unless you are compensating users for their time.

Capturing user information, details and behaviour patterns is only half the battle. What you do with that information is just as important. For more details, check out IDEA 19, *I've got your number.*

Try another idea...

'Your most unhappy customers are your greatest source of learning.'
BILL GATES

Defining idea...

'It is a very sad thing that nowadays there is so little useless information.'
OSCAR WILDE

Defining idea...

'I find that a great part of the information I have was acquired by looking up something and finding something else on the way.'
FRANKLIN P. ADAMS

Defining idea...

Q **Our sales manager doesn't want to send a questionnaire to customers without including some sort of promotion. She says it's a lost opportunity. Is this the right attitude?**

A *Every business is different and it may be that you have to combine the two, but adding a sales promotion, unless it's particularly attractive, is not going to help you get responses to the questionnaire – it will probably just confuse the message or get deleted without consideration. Better to offer an incentive to respond, with either a specific promotion or an electronic gift certificate.*

Q **All of our responses were very encouraging and not at all negative. Does this mean we have the perfect site?**

A *Unlikely. It just means your questions were loaded to receive positive responses or your sample was badly chosen. Have someone else create the questions and select a fair cross-section of your customer base.*

35

By whatever means necessary

Stop seeing customer complaints and suggestions as an annoyance and listen to what they're telling you. React to what they say by putting any problems right.

Some of them will of course be completely barmy — they might even be complaining to you about a product they bought from another company, but learn from your and other's mistakes.

TELL ME HOW MUCH IT'S HURTING

We all like to have a moan and vent our exasperation at times. The phenomenon of email converts even the most timid of us into raging, power-mad daemons. When things go wrong, web users will let you know in no uncertain terms, and the better web sites are those that don't shy from the rage but embrace it and, more importantly, learn from it. Your priority is to address the specific problem being raised, but you should also take an interest in finding the root cause of the problem/s and look to improve your overall service. You will receive a lot of nonsense (usually from residents of Idaho and Grimsby) and some rivals will even

Here's an idea for you... To see if users have a problem with communicating with you through your web site, test the system yourself. Set up a free web-based email account under a false name and write to the feedback address with a difficult but not obscure question about something on the site. How long until you receive a response (if at all)? Was your question answered and was the email polite? If you are not satisfied with all three points, look to improve this important service. If you had been a real customer/user, would you have been inspired to use the web site again? The response given to a user enquiry may be your only chance to hook them, so don't waste it.

throw in their tuppence worth, but that aside, these are the people who you are trying to impress with your site. They say that there is no smoke without fire, so if you are receiving a number of comments referring to failed deliveries or web site downtime, the chances are that something needs fixing, sharpish.

TELL ME WHY I SMELL

Offering users feedback forms is tantamount to setting yourself up for receiving untold amounts of complaints and random comments (as well as offers of marriage, employment, weight loss, etc.) But giving your users every opportunity to contact you – whether it brings good or bad news – is a shrewd move. Whatever your users decide to write, it's all valuable feedback; and making users spend more time on your site, crafting an email and thinking about you and your offering can only be a good thing. The processing of user feedback does come at a cost, but your users will generate many ideas, free of charge. Make sure you are offering them a feedback@ email address so that they can write to you, and more importantly, ensure that someone actually responds to these mails.

CUSTOMERS COME GOOD

Web site users prove their weight in gold when they are given half an opportunity to voice their opinion. Don't shy away from this pool of information and commentary. Show your contact details, whether that be a physical address, email address or telephone number. If any of these details are missing from the site, your customers might think that you have got something to hide (other than that photo of Aunt Nellie in the changing cubicle at Blackpool pleasure beach).

Customers prove particularly useful when it comes to:

■ **Policing the Site** – If there is any unsavoury content on your site (be it written by your staff or by other site users, such as on a message board – or that photo of Aunt Nellie) then it will be spotted. If the content is offensive or unsuitable, act quickly.

Bringing your customers in (albeit in a metaphorical sense) to help eradicate site errors and poor functionality is valuable after the site is launched, but much better to get their thoughts before you launch a new site or feature. To learn more about using testers, check out IDEA 6, *The acid test.*

Try another idea...

'*Programming today is a race between software engineers striving to build bigger and better idiot-proof programs, and the Universe trying to produce bigger and better idiots. So far, the Universe is winning.*'
RICH COOK

Defining idea...

157

Defining
idea...

*'There is a healthful hardiness
about real dignity that never
dreads contact and
communion with others,
however humble.'*
WASHINGTON IRVING

- **Broken Links** – It happens to every web site once in a while. A hasty build, a busy week or simply a customer following an out-of-date link – whatever the cause, customers will find them. Once you know about it, either fix the target page or remove the link.

- **Typos** – You've checked numerous times, but sometimes there's no escaping that typos do occur. Correct, and feel smug until the next one is spotted.

Defining
idea...

*'The creative act is not
performed by the artist alone;
the spectator brings the work
in contact with the external
world by deciphering and
interpreting its inner
qualifications and thus adds
his contribution to the
creative act.'*
MARCEL DUCHAMP

- **Product Information Incorrect** – Often, with large e-commerce web sites, product information is not authored in-house, but is provided by the manufacturer or wholesaler. Errors can occur, or information can be misleading. Often it takes one upset (and sometimes angry) customer to receive the item before you know that it's incorrect…again, appease the customer and make the corrections.

Q **I showed the results of the test to the customer services manager and received a curt reply (much like the email response) explaining that the customer's query was answered quickly. Would pursuing this matter not lead to me losing my job?**

How did it go?

A *The test is not supposed to be one department nitpicking with another – it's about empathising with your customers. If you thought your email query was not answered well or in a timely fashion, that's how your customers are going to see it. This needs to be fixed regardless of the personalities involved.*

Q **I was happy with the reply, but the response was a long time in coming. Customer services say they are inundated at the moment. What level of customer contact is normal?**

A *How long is a piece of string? Depending on what it is you are selling through the internet, customer contact will vary wildly. However, you can expect a response from between 5% and 10% of customers. Any lower is fantastic and any higher is going to be a real cost to the business in terms of resources.*

159

36

Area 51

There are the laws of the land, and then there are the laws of every other country in the world. Know what you can do – and where you can do it.

Toeing the legal line is time consuming and expensive — and necessary. But you'll need at least a couple of days out of the office to 'finalise the wording on this consumer contract'!

SORRY BOYS, NOT TONIGHT

The best place to start when trying to understand the maelstrom that is the law is to pay for the services of a lawyer or solicitor. Although you might still make a few mistakes, at least they won't be in the country that either you or your web site are based in – or if they are, at least you've got someone to blame.

The most obvious area to start discussions (and some would say the most fun) is with those sites that show or are intending to show images of a pornographic nature. The internet has done wonders for both the purveyors and viewers of pornographic images and the trend is unlikely to change. There is a tremendous amount of money in peddling porn, and although for some it's morally wrong, supply only exists where there is demand...But the law in many countries means that users must be over 18 to view these images – yet it's impossible to check this

Make contact with the government department responsible for trade to find out exactly what you should be aware of with regard to product regulations, age restrictions and countries currently affected by trade levies or embargoes. It is best for both you and your users if this information is made obvious on your site, rather than disappointing customers after they have placed, and paid for, an order.

information across the web. The best that you can do is to create an intro page that forces users to click to confirm that they are over the required age. By capturing the user's IP address, date and time of confirmation, a session ID and assigning all of this to their account (if your site charges fees or requires registration) will count as though you received a signature.

If you are selling weapons (or more likely kitchenware, especially knives), you must be clear on the minimum ages required by the laws of the countries you are intending to ship to. The same is true for selling toys on the internet if the toy includes small parts, toxic paint or carries a CE mark. Items and services that are more heavily monitored, and therefore require extra care in verifying purchasers, include alcohol, cigarettes, toxic products such as DIY material, and gambling or lotteries.

BUT SHOULD WE OFFER WORLDWIDE SHIPPING?

Not really. Whether you agree with it or not, most countries enforce trade levies or sometimes embargos on others. For the internet retailer or service provider, this has serious implications. As a UK- or US-based internet seller, for instance, you are simply

not allowed to trade with certain countries at certain times. The list is always changing, but the net effect is the same: some countries are off limits and therefore should not even appear in your shipping destination dropdown.

'The innocence of the intention abates nothing of the mischief of the example.'
ROBERT HALL

ELECTRONIC MAFIA

Selling electronic products or multi-media products is a real hornets' nest for the internet retailer. Electronic manufacturers know how to make money, and the best way to do it is to get the most you can, for each product, in every different country. You can't buy, say, a DVD player from the US and have it shipped to the UK. Why? Because electronics are much cheaper in the US and, combined with a favourable exchange rate (for the Brits anyway), the manufacturers know that they can make much more by blocking the export and charging UK consumers almost double for the same product. Check with your manufacturers or suppliers which regions you are allowed to sell into.

THIS IS MY PATCH!

It is not just the electronics giants that impose regional control. Many large clothing and apparel manufacturers act in the same manner, because it maximises profit. Often to sell a big brand you'll require retailer approval or even a contract to be allowed to buy and sell on the internet. It is highly unlikely that you'll be given world rights, at least initially, and you'll be told in no uncertain terms where you can ship the products to and where not.

There's a real lions den of laws and rules that any web site operator should be aware of. To learn more, check out IDEA 11, *Guilty until proven innocent.*

Try another idea…

'The power of hiding ourselves from one another is mercifully given, for men are wild beasts, and would devour one another but for this protection.'
HENRY WARD BEECHER

Defining idea…

'Man seeketh in society comfort, use and protection.'
SIR FRANCIS BACON

Defining idea…

How did it go?

Q   Our products are pretty innocuous – we sell beanbags – and my manager thinks that making contact with a government agency will only make us more likely to be badgered by them in the future. Isn't it likely that by contacting them we are setting ourselves up for needless checks in the future?

A   *Innocuous or not, you'll be surprised. Even beanbags are subject to certain regulations with regard to the fire-resistance of the filling and material. For the sake of a call, give it a go. Government agencies shouldn't record the nature of the calls, nor will it make you any more likely to be contacted by other agencies. Primarily they're there, don't forget, to promote trade and industry, not hurt it.*

Q   Surely all of this information is available online?

A   *The vast majority is, but sometimes a phone call to the right person can clarify points and lead to additional information you weren't even expecting.*

37

Who's the daddy?

Managing a web site effectively all boils down to control – but sometimes the best control is to put others in the driving seat and spread the responsibility.

Many hands make light work, but pushing the right button will also make the light work — show others the light switch but keep the fuse box locked tight.

WHO ON EARTH BUILT THAT?

Budgets dictate the amount of development that goes into a web site. If you're lucky there'll be an entire department at your beck and call, happy to lay down their life for the cause and unwilling to leave the office at night until the product is launched – but probably not. At best you'll have a dedicated team of developers or you'll be using a third-party development house for your coding needs. Steer away at all costs from build-your-own software, unless you actually understand the code behind the pages and can adapt it in-house. Running an IT department or hiring a third party does come at a cost, but the managerial control you'll have over the build, launch date/s and most importantly the quality of the end product is very high. Problems can be addressed quickly and before too much money has been spent, and last-minute changes are easier to implement.

Here's an idea for you...

Look to share some of the responsibility of running and maintaining the web site with other members of your organisation. Although some aspects should obviously remain in the domain of those qualified to act, get somebody from every department involved. This might mean creating an intranet where statistics such as visitor numbers, sales, revenue and expenditure can all be viewed securely, or it might mean a few printouts and a weekly site meeting. Whichever it is, if other members of staff feel empowered, they will get themselves (and maybe their teams) behind the initiative. Spread the load.

NOT MY PROBLEM?

This simple philosophy of sharing should not stop with the build or re-launch. It is important for tasks to be delegated throughout the company. The web site represents you all, and should not be the sole responsibility of one individual or department. Although some tasks will need a specialist developer or designer, Finance should be given a task within the commercial aspects of the site and the reporting; Marketing should be monitoring visitor numbers and be accountable for affiliate and advertising deals. The sales and merchandising teams should be looking at the conversion ratio (number of visitors to number of purchases) and pricing strategies; and the warehouse would do well to pay attention to the number of customer service contacts regarding shipments. In short, the web site, whether it's your only route to market or one of many, should involve everybody.

ROLLING ON

To really re-energise your web site everyone must buy into the concept, the potential and, of course, the end product. Only then will everybody's attention be focused on making the site a success. Involvement starts at the design and build of the site, and that means soft launching (or beta testing) before the site or new feature goes live. Use your staff mercilessly (along with trusted customers, if that's possible) to test and criticise and comment. Don't forget they all know the products and the business better than most – if even they can't suss the site, you have little hope...

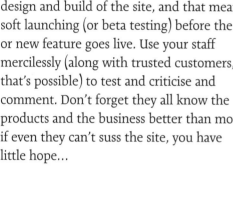

Regardless of who in the end takes responsibility for functions of the web site, there are some simple tricks to help keep your site operational, error-free and current. Check out, IDEA 42, *Chained to the kitchen sink.*

Try another idea...

'*So much of what we call management consists in making it difficult for people to work.*'
PETER DRUCKER

Defining idea...

'*Management is nothing more than motivating other people.*'
LEE IACOCCA

Defining idea...

'*Management by objectives works if you first think through your objectives. Ninety percent of the time you haven't.*'
PETER DRUCKER

Defining idea...

How did
it go?

Q   Our company is based across the country, so with an intranet we wouldn't be able to talk through the figures. How can we really replace the face-to-face meetings?

A   *Combine the two – organise a set date and time for a web site meeting, have all of the documentation posted on the intranet or a secure web page (or a simple Word/Excel document) and conduct a conference call. In this world of electronic communication distance should not be seen as an issue.*

Q   We are a traditional high street retailer. The sales guys argue that as they had no input in the look and feel of the web site they shouldn't be held accountable for sales. How can we get them back into the fold?

A   *The company's internet presence should be seen not as a separate function, but as extra sales channel that is as relevant as the high street branch. IT departments build great web sites but don't necessarily know about the products being sold on the site. Ask the sales manager what she would change on the site and look to implement the alterations. Meanwhile, insist that they take some responsibility – or hand over their commission for any web-based sales.*

38

Blind date

When it comes to building or updating a web site, many hands can make light work, but only if strict controls are in place. Singing, hymn sheets – it's all here.

Although it is a great relief to pass on responsibility and, let's face it, workload, onto others, there is a flip side. Don't let your flip flop.

CAN YOU HANDLE IT?

Administrative rights, or in simple terms, the power and ability to alter how information appears on a live web site, is a huge responsibility and not one that should be handed out without due thought. Although having multiple administrators means alterations and additions can be made quickly and in great numbers, you run the risk of more mistakes being made. Administrative rights should be handed out only when the recipient is absolutely clear of the responsibility she now has. If you can, set differing levels of admin rights, so that only experienced or qualified staff have full system rights and editorial staff (for example) are limited to text-only alterations. Make the gaining of permissions a rank-based right, rather than a staff perk. Not quite as attractive as a company car – but still…

Here's an idea for you...

For one week only insist that there is only one day (e.g. Monday) when alterations will be allowed to the site. Site administrators and content providers must spend the week before preparing the data they want to add/modify/delete and it is to be signed off by their line manager. To some, the extra checks might prove a little anal, but you'll be amazed by the number of faults the line managers will find with the material for one single build...and what would have been set live had you not put this check in place! Whilst the exercise simply cannot be repeated before every build, hopefully it will highlight to the content providers that errors occur on a regular basis. Future submissions, whether checked or unchecked, will be far closer to being error-free.

Defining idea...

'*Great services are not cancelled by one act or by one single error.*'
BENJAMIN DISRAELI

THREE TIMES A WEEK KINDA GUY

The size of your organisation and the number of products, services or articles you need to display on your web site will quickly determine how often you need to churn your homepage and category pages. As a rule of thumb it's best to have three set build days each week, ideally Monday, Wednesday and Friday. All the new copy and images can be prepared during the other days of the week, and for four out of seven days (especially the weekend) you know you'll have a stable site.

Concentrating the efforts of all the site administrators on specific days also means that if errors do occur, they can be quickly spotted and fixed. And all the appropriate staff are actually at work, or at least contactable.

CLEAN CODE

It is the responsibility of the IT manager or project manager looking after the site to set the house rules regarding style and code. There are many ways to achieve the same goals when it comes to code, but the stronger company is that which can achieve its goals in the cleanest possible way. Ensure that your code is as crisp as can be, that every line is essential and that your developers make the site as slick and effective as possible. When driving from A to B visitors don't want to take the scenic route. Keep it short and to the point.

It is always a lot easier to fix problems before they are live on a web site. To learn more about the art of checking copy, check out IDEA 41, *Publish and be damned.*

Try another idea...

WHO'S BEEN SLEEPING IN MY BED?

It is not healthy to be paranoid (but don't tell them), but there is nothing wrong with including controls in your system to ensure accountability and responsibility. Staff will change over the years, but your web site, hopefully, should survive these migrations. Have your developers, whether in-house or third party, document everything, no matter how obvious it all may seem. Someone else may have to pick the ball up when it's dropped and they will need as much information as possible.

When it comes to administrators using an interface to update the site, be sure to include an audit trail function, which is incredibly easy to implement and priceless for the information that it collects. Quite simply, if a change is made, the username is logged. This is not about instilling a big brother mentality; it's about considering your web site as being bigger than personalities. If a mistake occurs, anything that gives you the ability to specify and diagnose the problem is helpful. An audit trail works very quietly in the background and only comes to the fore when there's a problem.

'Quality has to be caused, not controlled.'
PHILIP CROSBY

Defining idea...

BARGAIN MANIA!

In reality, a few spelling or grammatical mistakes will rear their ugly heads on the web

'Watch out for the fellow who talks about putting things in order! Putting things in order always means getting other people under your control.'
DENIS DIDEROT

Defining idea...

171

site from time to time. Embarrassing yes, but hardly financially threatening. However, it is just as easy to make the potentially company-collapsing typing error known as mis-pricing. Mistakes with pricing product can cost you thousands, literally. The web community can be a far more close-knit group than you would ever imagine when it comes to a site posting the incorrect price for a product. Through email, news groups and blogs, the news that a site is selling at a ridiculously cheap price spreads like wildfire. As the provider, if you stick to the letter of the law, you are obliged to sell at the price advertised – although there have been a few high-profile cases where the provider has managed to explain it away as a mistake and offered the customers some meagre compensation instead of a DVD player for the price of a small bar of chocolate...

How did it go?

Q   **Our web manager says there is no way that we can only release new builds one day a week – our site has to be constantly altered to keep up with the competition. Can you think of something that will convince him to take part in this exercise?**

A   *Without conducting the checks and balances exercise at least once, you'll never know the level of errors being regularly uploaded to your site. The larger the site, the more likely mistakes will occur. Take the risk of a static site for a few days and understand the level of error.*

Q   **He still won't budge. What else can I suggest?**

A   *A little bit more draconian, but you could monitor each content provider individually. Instead of checking all content before it goes live, you could monitor just one provider each week, with their copy being proof-read by somebody else before it's put live. This won't interrupt your service as much, but will still prove the exercise. If that doesn't work, threaten to set fire to his beard.*

39

Message in a bottle

It's no good just hoping that visitors will learn about your site – you need to go out and attract them. Fortunately, there are ways and means of persuading them.

Gone are the days when 'persuasion' came in the shape of a lead-filled sock or leather cosh. Now you need more subtle ways to pressgang web users into paying you a visit.

TAG, YOU'RE IT

The simplest trick is to build metatags into the code of your site. Metatags are read by spiders and bots (programmes 'sent out' into the internet to pull in data for search engines) which, depending on what they find, will dictate how you appear on search engine listings – and to which of their users they will show a link to your site. By right clicking your mouse over your homepage and selecting 'view source', you'll be able to see the meta keywords as they exist now. They should be a list a words that relate to content or products on your site. But don't stop there, use variations of the same words, empathise with your user – if you sell CDs, as well as CD you should also spell out compact disc, as well as adding music, audio, tunes, etc. If a word is commonly mis-spelled, then include the mis-spellings in the metatags too. Capture as many people as you can through search engines, even if they are a tad illiterate (or bad at typing).

Find out what your metatags currently are, using the instructions given here, and try to double them. Use variants, plurals and mis-spellings. Give the search engines about four weeks to grab the new data and update their engine and you should then start seeing an increase in your traffic.

BE SEEN, BE SAFE

After metatags comes the fabled search engine maximisation. Some companies now operating offer only this service – for a very healthy monthly or annual fee they will ensure that your site is at the top of the major search engine listings. Although this service does give results to a limited degree, the process is fundamentally unsound as the same company could be working on behalf of numerous clients who are in competition with each other – and you can't all be number one! Far better to have your web site (even if it's database-driven) produce a static page for each and every product or service you have in your catalogue. The spiders and bots will see these pages and record them. Then, when a consumer is searching for something via a search engine, your specific product page can be seen, and at no additional cost.

I'M YOUR FRIEND TOO

An effective way to drive traffic to your site is to piggyback off other web sites that offer similar or ancillary products and services in the form of links. Who and what you are will quickly determine how much this is going to cost, but in principle you should be able to have a link to your web site on another site for very little if any cost. Ordinarily this will be a non-cash reciprocal arrangement, with you matching the link by adding a link to your new friend's site somewhere on your own. There is a limit to how many external links you

'I have noticed that the people who are late are often so much jollier than the people who have to wait for them.'
E. V. LUCAS

should place on your site – after all, you are in effect driving traffic away from yourself – but that limit is up to you.

PAYING FOR IT

Yes, the only way to really make sure you are receiving visitors is to throw some money at it…Advertising your web site, be it with banners, buttons, pop ups or links on other web sites, will drive traffic towards you. The downside is that any form of advertising is expensive, and you'll need to be clear how much you are prepared to spend, where and what you'll advertise long before you start to splash the cash.

A very clever middle ground is to offer an affiliate programme. This allows other web sites to be paid for driving traffic to your web site that ends in a proven sale – like a finder's fee. Your developers create affiliate IDs for your partners coded into the HTML and the host site places this unique link onto their web site, pointing either to a specific product or just to the homepage. If the visitor ends up purchasing, a percentage of the sale price is given to the referrer. Everyone's a winner.

Try another idea…

When planning an advertising campaign it is wise to look at how advertising would affect your own site. Any resistance you receive (or any astronomical bills) will be because the host web site is trying to maximise its revenue whilst minimising damage to its own offering. To learn more, check out IDEA 10, *Sell out loser.*

Defining idea…

'By a curious confusion, many modern critics have passed from the proposition that a masterpiece may be unpopular to the other proposition that unless it is unpopular it cannot be a masterpiece.'
G. K. CHESTERTON

Defining idea…

'Popularity? It is glory's small change.'
VICTOR HUGO

175

How did
it go?

**Q   IT added the extra tags and we did see extra visitor numbers, but
our conversion ratio fell. So, although we have more traffic, we
are still selling the same amount. What went wrong?**

A   *Be careful that the metatags you have added are actually relevant to the
site. Although millions of web users will search for the name 'Madonna',
you should only add this word to your metatags if you are providing
information or products relating to her or her music/films/books, or perhaps
selling religious artefacts. Trying to capture visitors by tricking them won't
endear them to your site, and although they will visit, a quick scan of your
homepage showing that you actually sell aquariums will mean they leave
again. The added words, if relevant, will bring extra traffic and the
conversion ratio should remain static.*

**Q   How can we use our existing visitors to find other like-minded
people?**

A   *Entice them with gifts or offers. If users enjoy your service, they may tell
others voluntarily. You can encourage this by offering them a gift certificate
or offer in exchange for forwarding someone else's details to you – but be
sure to only pay up once the new user has become a customer, i.e.
purchased something.*

40

Just here for the freebies

If a little of what you fancy does you good, just think how you'll feel when you get the whole package! Small free samples can lead to big sales.

Nothing is really free in this world — you should always get a return. If it's not cash, make sure its information — or a pair of pants, if that's your thing.

AS YOU REQUESTED

Fundamentally, the internet allows us to interact. Although most of the interaction is limited to reading words or looking at images on a web page, sometimes that just isn't enough. If you are selling products, then as well as providing the manufacturer's specification, you should try to replicate the user's experience in a physical store. This is easier for some products than for others. As a rule of thumb, if any of the aspects of physical world shopping can be shown through the web site, then you should try to include this representation online.

Here's an idea for you...

While you are looking into the copyright issues with manufacturers regarding downloads, to see just how effective and popular offering a download can be, create a document that you would like added to your site – this could be your company mission, your customer service charter, a list or diary of events, questionnaire or special promotional offer, whatever. Place the download link in a sensible and visible area of the site and monitor what happens. Users will download the document to read more if the download is interactive – such as a promotion or form that needs to be completed; a surprising number will come back to you.

Quite commonly it's a shrewd manoeuvre by internet sites to offer large printed material downloads for free on a web site. A great example is a user guide or any form of instructions. By offering a download you can shave hundreds, if not thousands, off admin costs by not having to pay staff or pay for raw materials such as paper and ink – let your users print out your material at their cost. Don't forget to ensure that the download or printable page is correctly formatted and 'printer friendly', otherwise your users will quickly get annoyed with wasting paper.

PLAY IT AGAIN

Obviously with recorded music or audio files there is a whole Pandora's box of copyright issues to be considered – and I'd strongly advise the employment of a copyright lawyer if you're even considering offering music downloads. But in principle, assuming you have obtained the copyright holder's permission, offering a teaser of what is contained on a CD is a great tool to use in selling an audio product. It can just be the first fifteen seconds of a few tracks, but that's all it takes. Suddenly the consumer knows exactly what she is getting for her money and you are protecting your revenue by not giving away too much.

NOW I'M HOOKED

Books or large documents of text (such as college exams or student's papers) also come with the same considerations regarding copyright, but again, in principle and with the

For more about offering
downloadable files and
ensuring your copyright, check
out IDEA 33, *You at the back,
stop copying.*

Try another idea...

right agreements in place, it should be possible to offer users a taster of what is contained within. At worst, a good bookstore should at least include the back cover blurb (or in the case of documents, the contents and maybe introduction) so that you are successfully replicating what the user would have had access to if she had the physical product in front of her in a store. Leave consumers with the need to read more and give them extra confidence that what they are looking at is indeed what they want. Providing too little information is mis-selling and only leads to more returns, so the revenue from those extra sales is soon lost.

PEOPLE LIKE YOU

In a bid to offer more of a community spirit some web sites have begun to use the data they hold on consumers and their buying habits as a feature on the site. Obviously you must always protect your consumers' actual identities, but you can show the most popular purchases based on what users from a certain country, or city, have bought. We all like to feel part of a group, and showing this somewhat innocuous information (which you already know; you just need to mine the data to find it) publicly can improve and influence sales in the most interesting of ways.

'When people are free to do
as they please, they usually
imitate each other.'
ERIC HOFFER

Defining idea...

'Sometimes when we are generous in small, barely detectable ways it can change someone else's life forever.'
MARGARET CHO

PRIVATE INVESTIGATOR

If information is your revenue, then it simply cannot be given away free of charge. But the same principles apply. Users and potential users need to know they are at the right place, and if there is a fee attached to accessing data (whether it's a paid-for download, streaming video/audio or plain text) they need to know that the information contained will be what they are looking for and worth the fee being asked. So show 'em. A small selection of information or examples work wonders – not enough to satisfy them, but enough to be able to make an informed decision. Once they've paid, issue the member/user with a unique customer login and ensure that the account is password protected.

'To know when to be generous and when to be firm – this is wisdom.'
ELBERT HUBBARD

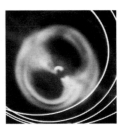

Q   **Marketing feels that offering a downloadable questionnaire is a little bit confusing. We're a web site-based company and want to be offering things like this online, not on paper. Won't this tactic dilute our offering?**

How did it go?

A   *That's a good point, but if you're not already offering the service online, and marketing would still like to learn the results of the questionnaire, then offering it in paper form is a start at least.*

Q   **Is there a way to remind users completing the questionnaire that we are a web-based company?**

A   *You can always tie-in the web site by printing a special web page address on the form, which would allow users who have completed the form, and sent it back, to enjoy a special offer or promotion.*

181

41

Inside the beast

Turn the internet around, point it at yourself and shoot. An intranet can be a real asset in most businesses, whether for human resources, disseminating information or ordering paper clips.

Intranets should not just be the domain of the technically minded. Encourage all your staff to get involved, even if it means threatening them with 'downsizing'...

DIFFERENT STROKES

When designing a web site that is pointing to the general public the basic maxim is that the site must be both usable and simple. This is very true for an intranet too, but you do have slightly more room for manoeuvre. The audience for your intranet are all your employees, so they will be far more willing than the general public to read longer documents (especially on company time). It should also be the case that all your employees are accessing the intranet through similar, if not the same, specification machines, enjoying the same connection speeds and with all the plug-ins, viewers and software required to fully utilise the information. This company-

Here's an idea for you... **If you don't have an intranet, start the ball rolling by creating a simple set of documents and building up from there. A great place to start is with basic information about staff. Sometimes entire departments, all working for the same company, never set eyes on each other. Although you must be careful about revealing staff members' personal contact information, some simple answers to standard questions, such as favourite film/book/pet can break the ice and show a far more sensitive, and artistic, side to the marketing director than anyone could have imagined!**

wide minimum specification is a wonderful gift for developers as it allows for better features and web-based applications that may not be rolled out onto the public web site for some time.

When designing an intranet it is generally accepted that you should start with a new design. Although certain elements, such as the logo, style of buttons and fonts, can remain the same, there should be some fundamental changes, such as colours and navigation, that make it quite clear to employees that the intranet is different, and therefore any information contained therein is not in the public domain.

ONE STOP SHOP

There really aren't any limits to what information can and should be included on your intranet. Everything from the names and biographies of new staff to the latest results in the company football league all deserve a place. Many companies are even trying to use the intranet as a way of eradicating company-wide emails, which seem a little superfluous now. Why write to every staff member with the same news and information and expect them to store it when you can just post it once, and leave the information on the intranet for users to retrieve whenever they need it! If you are going to place all company news, diary events and employee information on the intranet, it should be stressed to employees that it's their responsibility to access the intranet often (maybe set it as the default homepage) and it's your responsibility to ensure that all new documents and updates added to the intranet are clearly linked from the homepage and flagged for attention.

Ensuring quality and clarity of the information you post on the intranet is as important as what is posted on the web site. To find out more about the developing a house style and minimising errors, check out IDEA 16, *Style queen.*

Try another idea...

PROOF YOUR COPY

The rules of grammatical correctness and spelling are no less important on your intranet. Bad copy is quite simply bad for business – not only is it embarrassing that every employee will see another's failure to grasp the language, bad copy can prove to be confusing and waste the valuable time of employees who are trying to understand nonsense rather than getting on with their job. Check and check again, document everything and, much like with your web site, if possible have all copy proof-read by an editor.

'I'll publish right or wrong. Fools are my theme, let satire be my song.'
LORD BYRON

Defining idea...

'All you need in this life is ignorance and confidence; then success is sure.'
MARK TWAIN

Defining idea...

How did
it go?

Q   All good, but it's such an immense task. We want to create an intranet that fulfils a number of functions, but the IT department can't afford to take on an additional member of staff for the purpose. Is there a way round this?

A   *The beauty of intranets is that they can grow and grow. An intranet will take time to build, so every department must prioritise the features that are most important and build the intranet accordingly.*

Q   Populating the intranet is a massive job and IT say they can't cope. What can we do?

A   *Once the infrastructure is designed, the provision of content for the intranet can be sourced from the departments best served. So, human resources should be providing the information for their area of the intranet, customer services theirs and so on. Employing staff members specifically to look after the intranet is a resource that larger organisations enjoy, but for small to medium-sized firms, delegate!*

42

Chained to the kitchen sink

Make sure you are offering your users the best possible service and that everything accessible on the web site is both correct and relevant. Think spick, span and Bristol fashion.

Spring cleaning is all very good for a house (or car), but your web site is going to need tidying a little more often. Anybody know a good web site wash?

WHICH WAY NOW?

It might seem obvious, but if you are going to go to the trouble of creating a link or a button, be sure the link actually works. One of two things usually goes wrong: the code is modified and the link is broken or, more likely, the location of the destination page has been moved or deleted. Both are pretty embarrassing for a web site, especially if they are links from your homepage. Although developers (one would hope) will check that the links they create actually work, the chances are that the error or deletion happens to old links and that's why they go unnoticed. By occasionally checking links across the site you may catch a few errors; if not, rest assured that a user will eventually bring your attention to it – but better you find most yourself. You certainly want to avoid at all costs a 'friendly' email from a competitor drawing attention to your link failure…

Letting these jobs build up and only having an annual 'clean' will not only put you off ever doing them, it also means that any errors could have as long as a year to fester. Better to create a plan that means a little checking, often, involving as many people as possible.

Approach the department heads and explain that each area of the site has an owner – them. They can then nominate staff to be responsible for the information contained in those areas on the site. By involving as many people as possible it's much more likely that errors will be spotted (especially if you can engender a competitive element into the process), and it makes the job a lot more pleasant.

GET WITH THE PROGRAMME

I've said it before and I'll say it again – be extremely careful when you refer to dates in the future tense. April of next year might seem like ages away, but time stops for no web site and once the date has been reached and breached you're left with a daft sentence whittering on about forthcoming events or product releases that have already happened! Being clever with language and tenses eradicates the problem. If you want to draw your user's attention to the fact that a product will be released in 2007, say that it is available from 2007 – even when that date has passed the sentence will still make sense. This is true also of the copyright statement you may well have at the bottom of each page of your site. It must be someone's responsibility to alter the dates, keep them relevant and keep the copyright enforced.

WE WISH YOU A MERRY CHRISTMAS

Despite what views you and your company may hold about festivals and seasons, it's always a good move to acknowledge that many users place them in high regard, and alter their buying habits accordingly. You don't even need to alter the actual products or services that you're offering: grouping them under some kind of seasonal promotion will have an effect on what items are bought from your site and even the quantities. Show users that you've done the hard work and selected, for their buying pleasure, the most suitable items for Christmas, or summer, or Ramadan, etc.

LAST YEAR'S BLACK

To minimise the work and effort needed to keep your site in tiptop shape you need good procedural controls from the outset. For more information, check out IDEA 37, *Who's the daddy?*

Try another idea...

All services and products have a limited lifetime; rich indeed are the companies that can prolong this lifecycle forever. The net effect is that you'll be constantly updating your products and services to reflect demand, popularity and relevance. What happens to the older items? Well, if you want to provide your users with breadth of choice, then the old products simply become the back-catalogue. But if your warehouse space is limited, for instance, these products need to be removed from the site and all references to them eradicated.

NEWS FROM THE LAST CENTURY

If your site offers a chat function or discussion boards, then this can quickly clog your servers with material that is no use to man or beast, ever. The nature of discussion boards, especially if you offer a different forum for each different topic, dictates that the same material is constantly being discussed; the only thing that changes are the users taking part. Discussion and chat board users are very nomadic, and even hard-core participants will get bored and move on after about six months. Thus, there is no real need for you to offer users the chance to mine the messages from more than six months ago. By all means archive them, so that they are available should anyone feel nostalgic, but there is no real need for it to be public access, taking up valuable space and bandwidth on your servers.

'The greatest of faults, I should say, is to be conscious of none.'
THOMAS CARLYLE

Defining idea...

LOOKING FOR THAT SOMEONE SPECIAL

The language of the internet is a constantly changing phenomenon. Slang and acronyms are becoming acceptable and new technological developments mean new words – many of which may need to be added to your metatags. Back in 1998 if you were a web site offering digital images you could get away with mentioning a few file compression options such as .gif and .tif – but now, with so many competing software providers and file extensions, you could easily list way over forty. Constantly review and improve.

How did it go?

Q   Most of the department heads are throwing the job right back at IT as they are not empowered to make the alterations themselves. Surely it makes much more sense for the technical staff to both find the problems and fix them?

A   *That's a bit of a cop out. They must share the responsibility. The departments know their own business better than anybody – so asking IT to spot their errors is a bit stupid. It is much better for all concerned if the changes are submitted to IT and logged, ideally through the intranet. This way no change requests are lost or ignored, and there is an audit trail of who did what and when.*

Q   What is a good way to log errors and problems with the site, and ensure that they're fixed?

A   *You can either build a proprietary system as part of your intranet or, at a simple level, create an email address for staff to write to. The problem can be assigned to a member of staff to fix, and is only moved from the inbox when complete – don't delete it, save it to a 'fixed' folder.*

43

Piss up & brewery

Every page of your web site should allow users to travel very quickly to other areas of the site. Keep your navigation simple and clearly signposted.

Some customers are daft and most are very daft — always employ subtitles for the hard of thinking.

SO MUCH CHOICE

Where to place the navigational bar is a fundamental decision that is usually taken when your web site is first created. The nav bar is the top level of options open to users to allow them to surf seamlessly through your site. In the case of e-commerce sites the options tend to be your top-level product categories such as books, music, DVDs, etc. For service providers the options are far more varied, but the principle is the same. A firm of lawyers, for example, will break their site into the various areas of expertise, such as criminal law, family law, copyright law…No matter what the nature of your business all web sites should follow this model.

Now the next choice is where to place the nav bar. There are only really three options on offer: the left hand side of the page, across the top or straight down the middle. The choice is entirely yours and I believe that different sites lend

Here's an idea for you... Using the three potential options for nav bar placement (left hand side, across the top and straight down the middle), have your developers design three mock up pages to show what options are available and which one suits your site best. It might be, once alterations are made to colours, fonts and point size, that you immediately decide to launch a new version of the site. Good navigation should be the backbone of your web site; therefore it's not uncommon for the nav bar to completely lead and dominate the decision on how a site looks and feels. Note that having the nav bar down the middle of the page limits how much other material you can display on your homepage. I'd only seriously consider this option for a service industry or information-based site.

themselves much more to one or the other. Once you have decided on the location, this should be set in stone (at least during the life of this version of the web site). The number of options to offer? Remember the rules – simple and usable. Clear direction is needed, but not overindulgence. Keep it brief, but at the same time show all the options.

WHY BOTHER?

Good navigation on a site has a direct correlation to the number of pages a user will view on that site and the number of returning visitors, not to mention the number of consumers and therefore orders placed. Without good navigation, you may as well not invest in any more than a five page web site. Even if there are 15,000 plus pages, how is anyone going to ever see them if they can't get there in a logical and straightforward manner?

ALWAYS, ALWAYS, ALWAYS

Be consistent with your nav bar. Don't suddenly add or take away options at different parts of the site. Your user needs to get familiar with the layout fast and suddenly moving the nav bar from across the top of the page to the left hand side ain't gonna help. The same can be said for the options or buttons on the nav bar. You don't know which page a user will hit first. It isn't always your index or homepage – they could be following a link from your advertising, from a third-party site or from a friend. In a way, every page is your homepage, so it must contain as many of the constituent parts as is possible. The only excuse for removing or reducing the options on the nav bar is during the order pipeline because you want to ensure that the user becomes a consumer with the least amount of distractions possible.

AND THAT TAKES US TO?

Although it may seem obvious, buttons and links on the nav bar should go to the corresponding page of the web site. Be sure that the links work and that they do indeed point to the right destination. A useful technique to comfort users is to ensure that the target page has a heading that uses exactly the same title as appeared on the button taking them there. So, if your nav bar points to Financial Services, the heading on the page the user arrives at should say *Financial Services*, not *Insurance and Other Services* – or worse still, *Customer Services.*

Important as they are throughout the site, great navigational options are even more vital through the order pipeline to ensure the completion of the sale. To learn more, check out IDEA 50, *Stick that in your pipe and smoke it!*

Try another idea...

'*Success is relative. It is what we can make of the mess we have made of things.*'
T. S. ELIOT

Defining idea...

'*You're confusing product with process. Most people, when they criticize, whether they like it or hate it, they're talking about product. That's not art, that's the result of art. Art, to whatever degree we can get a handle on (I'm not sure that we really can) is a process. It begins in the heart and the mind with the eyes and hands.*'
JEFF MELVOIN

Defining idea...

'*The incompetent with nothing to do can still make a mess of it.*'
LAURENCE J. PETER

Defining idea...

How did it go?

Q   We think the alteration to the nav bar looks great. Marketing are keen to adopt the revised version as our homepage, but leave the rest of the site for a few months before implementing a new version of the web site. Surely this is OK?

A   *No, it isn't. Either make the alteration to the entire site or not at all. If the alteration to the web site has made marketing so excited, calm them down with a nice cup of tea and convince them that it's probably better to concentrate on finding the budget, time and resources to re-launch the site sooner than previously planned. In no circumstances should you launch just one modified page.*

Q   We have an e-commerce store but really like the idea of a central nav bar and little other text on the homepage. Surely the deeper navigational options can be introduced once the user has clicked through?

A   *This is bordering on an intro page, and makes your users decide immediately which path they want to follow from the outset. Far better to let visitors get a feel for your entire site through the homepage before moving on from there.*

44

You're in my manor now

Domain names are incredibly important; they can affect how well you will perform. Try not to choose a name that makes people snigger and point at you in the street!

It is essential that you protect your name and online brand with the same vigour and determination that you would a physical building — security, alarms and paying your rent on time...

THINK ABOUT THE FUTURE

Whilst all the psychology books will try to convince us that having a God complex is quite bad, there is something to be said for having a bit of ambition. Put simply, even if your business plan clearly dictates that you'll only ever operate in your home country for a predominantly domestic audience, don't let that stop you buying all the extensions you might want to use one day. If you meet any resistance from other staff, explain that it's better you own the other extensions than allowing a competitor to buy them and pass themselves off. Whichever domain names you eventually choose to buy, be sure to document the dates of renewal, and always buy the maximum amount of time that you can.

Here's an idea for you...

When I was at Amazon I was given a budget every week to buy books on the internet from our competitors. Why? Well, I'd like to believe that Amazon were incredibly benevolent employers and they knew how to retain a bibliophile; however, the real reason was much more clever, and nothing to do with me at all. Every Monday morning I would place an order with five competitors and over the week the orders would arrive. On each of the shipping notes/invoices there was a shipping number or reference – and all of these companies were using sequential numbering. So, for relatively little cost, we were able to see how many orders the company had ever shipped, calculate an approximate value of their entire business and see the number of orders they received a week – priceless.

If you use sequential numbering on your invoices/receipts – stop! Have this altered immediately; someone out there is monitoring your business. If you can, place some orders with competitors and see if they are – this intelligence is frightening, both in terms of what you can learn about your competition and how easy it is to obtain.

THERE ARE NO RULES

You might feel morally ambiguous about this, but wise indeed is the company that puts out a search on competitor domains with a view to buying them up as soon as they lapse. Now it probably would be somewhat immoral to keep hold of those domain names should they enter your possession and deny another company (even if they are a competitor) the ability to trade through their own site – but just the act of giving them back, not-for-profit (well, if I must), is a magical PR opportunity that is well worth the tiny investment. Let's face it; there may be thousands of people trying to do exactly the same to you...

If you want people to shop at your site again and again they must learn to trust you. You'll achieve this over time mainly by offering a good web site and good service. If users like your site they will tell their friends and the cycle will begin once more. So you have built up a strong brand (www.clampcity.com) that people trust and then some low-life competitor buys up the same name with a different extension (www.clampcity.net). What they end up doing with this domain name is irrelevant – but it will cause you to lose customers, either because their service is better or because it's worse and it mistakenly reflects on you.

As well as constructing and maintaining a brand that users feel comfortable visiting and spending money with, you can help keep your visitors attracted by making them feel part of a larger community. For more information, check out IDEA 46, *There's no place like home.*

Try another idea…

ANOTHER DOT SOMETHING

New extensions are being created pretty much every year. Some are simply ridiculous (.me.uk) and some are very clever (.tv). But you must stay on the ball and pre-order your domain with the new extension as soon as you can. It is, of course, possible to 'win' back domain names from companies or individuals obviously 'passing themselves off' in a court of law, but why go through the hassle when, for the price of a sandwich, you can register the name yourself? Domain names have dropped in price considerably and will continue to do so. Shop around for all the domain names that you may possibly want to use in the future; even if you never get round to building anything, it stops others using that name.

'There is always more spirit in attack than in defence.'
TITUS LIVIUS

Defining idea…

Defining idea...

AND?

It is not uncommon for company names to include the word 'and' or include an '&'. These company names were usually formed long before the internet was a glint in the scientist's test-tube. The knock on effect is how is the name represented as a domain name? The options include:

- www.clamp-company.com
- www.clampandcompany.com
- www.clamp_company.com
- www.clamp&company.com

The answer? You will have to buy them all and point them towards your main site (the site address or URL you use in promotional literature).

Q **It looks like our competitors have got wise and decided to adopt coded shipping numbers. Our numbers guys are questioning how useful the exercise is for us. Do you think they've got a point?**

How did it go?

A *Even if you are unable to determine your competitors' sales figures, you can still mark them on other points. You can monitor their ability to confirm your order/s, confirm despatch and follow up on any customer service queries you may have; and if you return the product/s, how good is that aspect of their service?*

Q **Will ordering from competitors tell us anything else?**

A *You will also be able to see what, if any, marketing deals have been struck with third parties. Are there any flyers contained in your delivery advertising banks, or credit cards, etc.? Where else are your competitors earning revenue and can you do the same?*

45

The missing link

How do you link effectively without diluting your own site? Answer that question and you will be on your way to a busy and prosperous web site.

Only link with companies you are happy to be seen in public with. Would you want to introduce Company X to your mates — or worse, your mum?

A very quick way to start driving traffic towards you is to ask, or pay, other web sites to put a link to your site on theirs. More often than not, this means adding a link to an external site in return...So where do you draw the line between exposure for yourself and diluting your own offering?

RUB MY BACK

The ideal way to link effectively without diluting your own offering is to insist on a prime position on their site, but not to return the favour – i.e. hide the reciprocal link somewhere in the dark depths of your web site. But you aren't likely to get away with this too often. As a compromise you can create a links page, either found from the homepage or through the nav bar, which will simply list all the web sites

Here's an idea for you...

Define the space on your homepage that can be freed up for external linking/advertising (don't choose the absolute bottom of the page because the offering won't be attractive to potential partners). Contact five partners whom you feel are not in direct competition with you but who have related products (and standards). Tell them that this is a new initiative and that if they become early adopters they will receive more impressions for the first six months if they join up now. This will quickly prove if the initiative works for your site, and meanwhile a well-placed link will be driving traffic to you from five reasonably large customer bases.

that you have these agreements with. Again, the 'partner' web site may insist that their link is given a prime position, if that is what you expect in return, and there may be no getting away from the fact that your homepage is going to have more links to external partners than it does to information or products contained within your web site. This is a problem, a huge problem. No matter how many visitors are being shepherded to your site, unless you are keeping them there, then the whole exercise is a little bit pointless. Choose your deals wisely.

GYRATE YOURSELF

A way round this conundrum is to offer your partners something better than a link in return. But that doesn't make sense, I hear you cry. Oh yes it does. In essence you are offering to repay a link to your site with a graphic, prominently displayed on your homepage. What's the catch, you (and most probably they) will ask? Well, you'll set up this relationship with a number of partners. Because you have dedicated so prominent a portion of your homepage (the most valuable web real estate there is) to them in return for a simple link, they won't complain if you rotate the adverts/links between partners. Each unique visitor will see only one of the links available, but no matter how many relationships you set up, the space dedicated to promoting other sites will never alter. You can afford to expand without diluting your offering any further.

BE CAUTIOUS

Do be careful with links – both when you accept links on your site and when you post them on others. What those companies do in terms of ethics, morals and customer service will reflect badly on you if your sites and companies appear to be linked in any way.

A POSITIVE SPIN

Linking does lose you users, but the benefits usually outweigh the negatives by far. With enough links out there you'll be bringing traffic to your site, and that traffic may well find exactly what they are looking for right there, on your site. Without the links you wouldn't have received the extra business. Linking, and finding a place on the internet, is all about creating a community – be that with your consumers or with the other companies you choose to partner with. A sign of success is reducing the number of links you have to others on your site, and that is something that will happen over time – but until then it is often a necessary evil.

Promoting yourself online is a delicate balance between what you are doing offline to increase awareness and what you are doing on the site itself to ensure that the right message is being conveyed. To learn more, check out IDEA 2, Look at me!

Try another idea...

'We've heard that a million monkeys at a million keyboards could produce the complete works of Shakespeare; now, thanks to the internet, we know that is not true.'
ROBERT WILENSKY

Defining idea...

'Friendship makes prosperity more shining and lessens adversity by dividing and sharing it.'
CICERO

Defining idea...

How did
it go?

Q **The web sites that are agreeing to the project aren't really our first choice as their visitor figures aren't as high as we'd hoped. Our sales manager thinks we're wasting our time. Is she right?**

A   *This exercise is never a waste of time. The results will always tell you something. In a way it's important that everyone manages their own expectations. It's impossible to avoid the effect of ego when it comes to running web sites. At the end of the day, sites that feel they need to offer links in return for leaving a few of their own still need to grow. This is not a bad thing, just a natural part of growing an internet business.*

Q **We have targeted ten sites with whom we would like to set up reciprocal links. How many of these sites will agree?**

A   *Don't ask me – ask them! Seriously, the sites that will first take you up on the offer will be the smaller sites – desperate for any growth. As you become bigger yourself, the less need you'll have for reciprocal links. But until then, it will always be a matter of the weak helping the weak.*

46

There's no place like home

If you can create a community feeling on your site you'll reap the rewards in terms of numbers of visitors and consumers, whatever you are selling or promoting on the web.

What you really want to do is replicate the Beano fan-club and give all of your users a badge, fact sheet and free poster — they'll love you for it.

A HOME FROM HOME

When it comes to comfort, we would all much prefer a soft and luxurious hotel duvet than a starchy, stained motel blanket. This is the feeling you need to replicate for users. Envelop them in your expertise and knowledge, convince the world that your web site is the definitive provider of information or products, and give them a nice warm feeling that makes it nigh on impossible for them to leave. (A courtesy bar of soap would probably help, too.) When users feel relaxed and at ease they will automatically want to spend more time on your site, and if there is something to buy, then hands will be reaching into wallets. And never underestimate the power of word-of-mouth. With the propensity of chat rooms, discussion boards, email and

Here's an
idea for
you...

Look on the web and find some shareware message boards that can be downloaded. Compare the specifications, especially the ability to customise, the appearance (if any) of third-party advertisers and any need for users to have to download a plug-in to take part. Once you've found some suitable software, add it to your site. You can hide it from public view until you have configured it and tested its functionality. Don't think message boards are only suitable for b2c (business to consumer) web sites. They can be incredibly effective additions to b2b (business to business) sites too, by allowing clients to post messages to other clients.

blogs – it does not take long for news to get around. Users will be so impressed with your site and your service that they'll tell all their friends. It's time to go to the cash & carry for your toiletries order...

LET'S SEE WHAT'S NEW

You want people to leave feeling that they simply must come back. Taking Granny hostage is one way, though a little risky. Instead, create fresh content. Be it once a week, day or hour it will cost, but if users get used to seeing fresh, dynamic information every time they log on, it's only going to encourage them to keep doing it. Make your users feel they have to come back in case they're missing out on something. What's new then becomes hot news, which will quickly spread. Now sit back, pour yourself some Sauvignon Blanc and relax as others fervently pass on links to your web pages.

WITH BONUS DISK

To kick-start your web site into becoming a community site, both for hard-core aficionados and the casual browser, you really need to win their hearts and minds, and get one up on the competition. A quick way to win (though not necessarily cheap) is to ensure you have the hottest gossip, forthcoming products or news. By making arrangements with manufacturers or sending your roving reporter out into the field, the quickest and most effective way of building a name for yourself is to be the one site that provides that little bit of extra information for users. If you can tie it in with a competition or promotion where new registrants can win an exclusive or limited-edition product unobtainable anywhere else on the web (or in the world), word will spread quickly and you'll be well on your way to creating a community.

AIR YOUR VIEWS

The most successful web communities are those that welcome and even encourage user interaction. Allowing users to vent their anger, sing praises, generally have a moan or even search for romance is a winner. With the proliferation of software and applications, and with a developer who knows his PERL, you can even download some for free off the internet and have a fully tailored, operational message board on your web site in a matter of hours. The amount of resources you use to run your chat service or message board is entirely up to you; you can actually get away with none at all. But it's always best to have a moderator or two to keep tempers checked and language appropriate. This is where the users come in again; offer the job (unpaid) to your early adopters and most will lap it up. Amazing, but true.

Building a community around your web site means coming into contact with a lot of information from users. To learn more about using that data, check out IDEA 19, *I've got your number.*

Try another idea...

'My favorite thing about the internet is that you get to go into the private world of real creeps without having to smell them.'
PENN JILLETTE

Defining idea...

'On the internet, nobody knows you're a dog.'
PETER STEINER

Defining idea...

'Without a sense of caring, there can be no sense of community.'
ANTHONY J. D'ANGELO

Defining idea...

How did it go?

Q **Although the developers were able to customise the message board, we would rather it was branded like the rest of our web site. So IT is going to budget for a proprietary system and wait to launch next year. Is this going to work?**

A *Certainly keeping brand recognition across the site is very important, but you'll find that most message boards look the same – boring grey background, a few icons and lots of text. But that's the point – they are tools to allow users to post and read messages.*

Q **Won't it look boring and put users off using it?**

A *By the time users have customised their account with a graphic that is supposed to be them, the page will be fairly alive with graphics and, more importantly, text. The banner that lies across the top of the page is pretty secondary as far as they're concerned. Launch the free version now, treat it like a test phase and spend the year building your own. In a year you'll have a ready-made community that you can just transfer across.*

47

News from the front

High street shops and offices involve physical contact; web sites don't. Making users feel special by positive interaction, information or rewards can go a long way to restoring the balance.

Giving your customers a stroke every now and again will bring in the repeat business. Don't worry — your firewall should stop you contracting any nasty illness...

I DIDN'T KNOW YOU WERE A BLOGGER?

Adding a weblog (or blog) to your site will only suit certain businesses, but if the hat fits, wear it with pride. The beauty of weblogs is that they can contain absolutely anything, no matter how obscure or irrelevant. There is a bit of a buzz attached to creating a blog and knowing that your words, no matter how off the cuff, are being read on the internet. As readers, we feel that we are really getting into the mind of the author and will often read for far longer than we would on the regular part of the web site because the language is chattier and less sales orientated. Do consider adding a blog to your site, whatever it's about (a place to start if you're stuck is 'A day in the life of...'). Get someone senior (or someone who's willing) to spend twenty minutes of their working day updating their blog (instead of playing solitaire). Some of your users will be fascinated.

Here's an idea for you... **Encourage the IT department to add a blog to your web site. You can hide it from the public until it's fully operational and contains plenty of content. Rather than dictating that a certain member of staff writes the blog, have staff volunteer for the role (multiple authors for the same blog is fine) and watch how it progresses. If the content is suitable and no company secrets or damaging office gossip are being revealed, set the blog live.**

WELCOME TO OUR WORLD

Users are also interested in hearing news from the frontline. Now, some information will obviously be highly sensitive or under NDA (non-disclosure agreement) – like the MD's latest pay increase and/or redundancy proposals – but if you are able to, reveal or just hint at what deals may be in the pipeline, forthcoming advertising runs, staff successes – even details of your manufacturers' and suppliers' forthcoming products if you're privy to them. It all helps in the war to win visitors. The key is to make the news accessible, personal and current.

A VAST IMPROVEMENT

Fans of your site will also want to be kept informed about changes to it. There are two audiences that you'll have to cater for: the 'techies' and the 'owners'. The 'techies' will be very keen to learn about any improved bandwidth, servers, features and functionality that your web site will be getting in the near future. If you can release actual technical details, they will lap it up. The 'owners' are those users who feel they have been around so long, and are so important to the continued success of your web site, that their presence is the actual backbone of the company. They too will want to know about forthcoming features and improvements (though maybe not in such detail), and will probably contact you to let you know what they think about it all. Sometimes amusing, but always useful – these users are providing valuable feedback.

WHAT CAN YOU DO FOR ME?

Keeping users truly happy does mean treating your loyal customers and registered users with the occasional perk or special offer that both acknowledges and rewards their continued presence on your site. Don't think that you have to give anything away for free (although acts of benevolence will certainly help) – offering your chosen few a chance to shave some money off their next purchase through an electronic gift certificate, removal of shipping fees or access to limited edition or cheaper products will do just as well. All of these tactics mean another sale for you, and your user feels loved and appreciated.

As well as adding some nice to have features to a site, you need to make sure that the entire site is clear in both what it wants to achieve and how information is presented. To find out more, check out IDEA 15, *Looking good tonight!*

Try another idea...

STROKING YOUR CUSTOMERS

One very successful technique to encourage users to visit, buy and keep coming back is to offer customer accolades. Offer users the chance to comment on products they have bought and then acknowledge the best review with a reward. Alternatively, in a bid to get lots of user-created content on your site fast, reward the most active reviewer/poster and show a league table to encourage competition and output.

'The meeting of two personalities is like the contact of two chemical substances: if there is any reaction, both are transformed.'
CARL JUNG

Defining idea...

'I want freedom for the full expression of my personality.'
MAHATMA GANDHI

Defining idea...

211

How did
it go? **Q**   **Our sales manager thinks that users who would have bought products might spend their time on our site reading the blog instead. As she says, our web site is there to sell stuff. Is she right to think like this?**

    A   *This is a bit of a 'sticky' point, actually. The blog won't directly increase sales, but nor will it diminish them. Adding the blog allows users to feel more comfortable with your site and your offering. If the user learns to trust you by getting to know you, it will help sales indirectly.*

    Q   **Is there a different way to achieve the same aim without adding a weblog?**

    A   *You can always add a static page, such as 'Webmaster's Message', but be sure to update it as often as possible.*

48

I'm a believer

How do you turn a visitor to your site into a consumer? Make them welcome, put them at ease, make yourself attractive, make ordering simple...oh, just read!

Your site is not there to look pretty; it's there for a reason — to make money. Unashamedly pimp your site and don't let your working pages go to sleep on the job, so to speak.

THE ROAD TO DAMASCUS

If you want to understand why not every visitor ends up buying from you, remind yourself of your own surfing behaviour. Not everyone on your web site is going to buy, and there's nothing you can do about it. First, there are going to be visitors to your site who really are just looking, for whatever reason. Secondly, there will be visitors who found you by complete accident (probably via a link on a search engine) and don't know where they are going or why they are there. Some will scan your homepage and leave immediately, while others will have a quick read because something caught their eye, but they won't become a consumer. With average

Here's an idea for you...

If you're running an e-commerce store, make a direct comparison with your competitors' or with the manufacturers' own web site with regard to how data are presented. Are you really giving all that you can in terms of information and images? More importantly, are you adding to that information in any way by giving the users a chance to read more than the specification – will they enjoy this product, will it improve their lives, will it make them laugh? All quite simple, but add these features and you'll notice an increase in your conversion ratio.

If you are selling services rather than products, have your copy checked over by an outside source. Is it absolutely clear what is being offered, how much it costs, how long the service will last and why buying the service from you is more advisable than from another source? If not, fix it and see your conversion ratio increase.

conversion ratios of anything between 1% and 5%, how can you ensure that you are at the top rather than the bottom of this scale (or even on it at all)? Well, when you visit a web site, what dictates whether you end up buying? As we'll see, a number of factors come into play.

BIG BRAND, LITTLE BRAND

Brand awareness will eventually happen over time, through trust (maybe of a parent company, or sympathetic PR) or because it's bought through a massive advertising campaign with a budget that would make your eyes water. Branding does take time, but once your brand is established it will help users become consumers just because of what you are.

GIVING IT UP

A major complaint from users, when they're not chasing their orders, is lack of information. Although it's important to keep web copy to a minimum, there's no excuse for not including basic information about the products you are expecting your users to buy with their hard-earned cash. If users are asking you for more information, you can be sure that only a small proportion are actually parting with their pennies. Most of the others, myself included, would be off to another site where the information is more freely available. Net result, lost business. All for not repeating verbatim what has been provided to you from the manufacturer or supplier. Very poor indeed – nul points.

The order pipeline is hugely important in the race to convert users into consumers. To learn more, check out IDEA 50, *Stick that in your pipe and smoke it!*

Try another idea...

WHERE EXACTLY AM I?

Users will feel a lot happier spending time on your site and buying from it if they can work out how to get around it. It's back to ensuring that you have good navigation, and links and buttons that not only work but take users exactly where they want to go quickly and seamlessly. Improve your site navigation and you'll see a rise in your conversion ratio.

'The internet is so big, so powerful and pointless that for some people it is a complete substitute for life.'
ANDREW BROWN

Defining idea...

Defining
idea...

THAT'S ILLOGICAL, CAPTAIN

The order pipeline and the buying process itself can scare a lot of users away, even though up until then you had them hooked on you and your products. It defies belief that organisations spend so much time and effort (and therefore cash) designing the ultimate site in terms of attractive navigation and well-presented products, only to let themselves down spectacularly with the final, most important step – the shopping basket and order pipeline. You should spend as much time and effort on the design and implementation of your order pipeline as on your homepage. Getting users to select products or services from your site and putting them into a basket or cart is only half the battle. You now need to get them to walk through the checkout without dropping the purchase and scurrying off into the distance with their purse clenched tightly to their chest.

Q   **Our competitors have got the product information section of their site perfected. They even have a facility to let users who have bought in the past to comment on the products. Our IT department says we haven't got the budget to add a similar facility to our web site. Any ideas how we can compete?**

How did it go?

A   *So your competitors have got it right. It does happen. But don't give up. Instead, try to match their level of 'this is how it really is' by adding your own staff comments to products within the product description. This way, users will see both the official manufacturer's blurb and, immediately below it, a few hundred pragmatic words from Jack in customer services saying how much he liked it. No expensive applications required (no offence, Jack). You have staff working at your company and they are all consumers...use them.*

Q   **Should we still allow users to phone their orders through? Our biggest competitor does.**

A   *Ah – this is a case of keeping up with the Phoneses! It depends on whether you can handle the contact time. More and more people every day are becoming familiar with e-commerce so there is really less need. A good tactic is to add a surcharge for telephone assistance to help 'educate' your users (and pay for the extra resources you have just thrown at it).*

49

The importance of being lazy

To truly re-energise your web site you must pass the donkey work back to the site, its supporting databases and your back-end systems. Maximise your time and let the technology take the strain.

A happy technology is a labour-saving one.
So cheer your web site up and use it properly.
Now repeat: I will be lazy, I will be lazy, I will be lazy...

IT'S ALREADY THERE

Other than updating and improving the web site, which is a full time (and often a team) role, your web site should be looking after itself and leaving you time for a spot of golf (I mean more time to attract visitors and ship orders for existing customers). With good back-end systems you should be able to capture all the data you want, and then be in a position to interrogate that data in any fashion that suits you. When customers order or register with your web site they leave bits of information behind, not least their email address. This amounts to nothing less than a self-building mailing list that comes free of charge, from people who are

Here's an idea for you...

Through your own database/s find out which sites are referring visitors to you and in what quantities. Make a list or even a graph showing where people are coming from and, in the case of search engine referrals, what those users are actually typing to find you. First, check to see if all of those words are contained within your metatags, and if not, add them. And secondly, approach the marketing department with the proposal for a targeted advertising campaign on the search engine that is best serving you already, using the statistics you have to support your argument.

already interested in you. Assuming that you offer an opt-out facility, all the email addresses left on your records have agreed to be contacted at a later date about your offers and promotions – so go for it.

Your back-end systems should also be able to tell you who ordered what, and when. Your customer service team needs only to access the data to answer any phone or email queries straight away.

Some deeper data mining will soon reveal obvious trends, from the most popular items and downloads to sales patterns, by day, by month or season. What you do with this data is very much determined by what sort of company you are and what resources you can devote to analysing it. But the last thing that should happen is for the data to be completely ignored.

Your databases will also have the location recorded for every shipment sent from your warehouse. If you marry this information up with the average amount spent in these areas, you'll soon be able to create a customer map and can advise marketing where it would be best to advertise (they'll like that!) and what sort of return you can expect.

Finally, an often overlooked piece of information that you should be capturing is the referral page that brought users to your site. By capturing the referrer you'll be able to see where users were last and, in the case of a search engine referral, the exact word or phrase (including typos!) that

If you want to learn more about how to position yourself on search engines and fully utilise your metatags, check out IDEA 39, *Message in a bottle.*

Try another idea...

the user typed to find you – absolutely priceless. From this information it becomes very obvious which of the links you have set up are actually working and which search engine is serving you best.

EVERYONE GETS A PLAY

To maximise your staff's effectiveness on the web, it's important to provide the necessary tools, and not to assume any technical knowledge. If you have the right GUI (Graphical User Interface) in place any idiot can update a web site (although it's best to leave the idiots out of the process if you can; someone's got to run the company) with absolutely no technical knowledge or understanding of the processes going on behind the scenes. Any jobs that IT can pass on to other departments will both make your site more effective and reduce the number of errors. If an editorial team is responsible for creating most of the site's content, go the extra mile and give them the power to update the content live on the web. Having the information piled up for IT staff to add is counterproductive: if they can concentrate on making improvements to, and launching new features for, the web site, it is better for the company.

'Ambition is a poor excuse for not having sense enough to be lazy.'
EDGAR BERGEN

Defining idea...

'Progress isn't made by early risers. It's made by lazy men trying to find easier ways to do something.'
ROBERT HEINLEIN

Defining idea...

Q **The marketing department really appreciate the stats but argue that the search engine site I want them to target with a campaign is already providing a healthy amount of traffic for our site. Why pay them?**

A *If you leave it alone, the chances are your visitor numbers will increase slightly (especially if you alter your metatags to reflect the areas you had missed) without your company spending a penny. But you are not looking for status quo (they hardly tour nowadays anyway), you are looking for growth.*

Q **Our CFO wants to know if we should stick with one search engine or spread ourselves around. What shall I tell her?**

A *If the majority of users are finding you through one particular search engine then you can assume that your customer base will tend to favour this search engine on the whole. By investing in a targeted campaign you'll be appealing to other like-minded individuals who are far more likely to visit you, and ultimately consume.*

50

Stick that in your pipe and smoke it!

The order pipeline is like an underwater breathing tube. If it gets a kink or is blocked – you know you are in trouble.

Make the ordering process problem-free for the customer and don't let them leave without spending some money!

Despite marketing attracting new visitors, merchandising placing the right products at the right price, and sales and editorial presenting them in the best possible light – if users find it difficult to actually buy from you, it will all have been in vain.

JUST BAG IT UP

The act of a user placing an item into their shopping basket and the consumer's path to purchase is often referred to as the order pipeline. This is the distance and number of pages a consumer must face before their choice/s of purchase become their own. Just as good web design is all about offering both simplicity and usability, an effective order pipeline is equally short and to the point. If you had to complete an obstacle course every time you went to the supermarket, you would soon look for an alternative (unless training for the steeplechase). The same is true for web sites.

Here's an idea for you...

Look at your order pipeline as it stands and map out the process using only half the number of pages to get a customer from basket to completion. A tall order, but an important step in learning that not every question is essential to getting this customer's product delivered to them. With the new process mapped out, approach IT and try to get your changes implemented. If you're successful you'll see an immediate increase in your conversion ratio.

JUST THE BASICS, PLEASE

When designing or re-designing your order pipeline look to shave off as many stages as possible between a user selecting what they want to buy and the order confirmation page. You need to look at your current set up and define which details are important for this order and which can be captured later. If you have the time and the tools, look at how many customers place an item in their basket and how many complete their order. The lost custom is absolutely heartbreaking. You will probably be losing about 50% of your custom for every page of the order pipeline. So, if a hundred people put an item into their basket and there are five pages of order pipeline, you'll end up at just over three orders actually being completed (and who wants an eighth of an order? Where's the profit in that?). Imagine the difference if you take away two of those pages. Suddenly you'll be enjoying over twelve orders per hundred instead of just three.

Defining idea...

'Manifest plainness Embrace simplicity'
LAO TZU

CALLING THE SUPERIOR

Even if your order pipeline is perfect, there are some delays that you simply can't get rid of and the main culprit is bank confirmation of the customer's card details. Although you can't speed this process up, you can let your consumers know what's going on. Even if it's as simple as showing a sand timer or a message, explain that the site is still working, just looking for information from another source.

Likewise it's probably worthwhile offering a phone or fax number for people to leave their credit card details. Although the fear has gone from most web users about the security of their card details, there are still some customers who feel safer reading their card number to a human being. You are quite within your rights to charge a surcharge to cover the associated administration costs.

The order pipeline is only part of the navigational choice you offer on your web site. To perfect the rest, check out IDEA 43, *Piss up & brewery*.

Try another idea...

'Simplicity is the peak of civilization.'
JESSIE SAMPTER

Defining idea...

'It is simplicity that makes the uneducated more effective than the educated when addressing popular audiences.'
ARISTOTLE

Defining idea...

Q **We understand the importance of reducing the number of questions we ask of users, but that said, we're worried that if we don't ask for this information at the order stage, we'll never get the chance to capture it later. Are we missing something?**

A *The answer is simply to explore what information marketing want to capture and how essential it is to shipping the product. If the information is being captured for potential future projects, such as asking for a mobile phone number, then this question needs to go.*

Q **Is asking for a telephone number surplus to requirements?**

A *No. A single number is useful in case you ever need to contact the customer, but don't go overboard and ask for a home, work and mobile number, the number of a good plumber...*

51

The sound and the celluloid

By using sound files and movie files you can wow your visitor and get your message across quickly and effectively. So plug in and turn on...

The eyes and the ears are the way to your customer's wallet....

SONIC BOOM

Using sound on your web site can give you two means of communication running simultaneously – the user can listen to the sound (it can be music or speech) and read the text on the page. If you get it right, you can impress your user visually and aurally.

The most common use of sound on a web site is when interactive noises are 'created' when the user clicks on a link, a button or a new screen. But don't overdo it. Although there is a novelty factor associated with a high-pitched scream every time we use a button, it quite soon wears very thin. As soon as your hilarious sound becomes an annoyance you'll be driving visitors away. Likewise, overpowering users with too many gimmicks (whether audio or video) can be counter-productive. The last thing you want to instil is confusion.

Here's an idea for you...

If you're currently using audio or video files on your site try converting some of the most important or popular ones for use with different viewers/players, and offer a low-res and hi-res option. Have your developers add a traffic monitor to each of the links and after maybe four or five weeks you should have enough data to determine your users' most popular choice of viewer/player and preferred resolution. Be sure to offer some players that are not Microsoft products, such as Real Player and QuickTime.

The effective use of sound can show users the personality or personalities behind a web site. Whether this is a comic exchange, the managing director's report to the AGM or satisfied customers advocating the use of your products and services – they all give weight to what it is you are trying to achieve.

WHITE NOISE

If you're going to do something, make sure you do it properly. The decision to use sound should go hand in hand with the decision to use the best quality sound files you can. In this age of digital audio, there really isn't any excuse for poor recordings. To minimise problems with quality, it's worth recording the audio digitally in the first place (if possible) rather than trying to convert later.

Defining idea...

'Of all noises, I think music is the least disagreeable.'
SAMUEL JOHNSON

Any large audio file (say, more than 30 seconds of music or 1 minute of voice) should be options that the user chooses to listen to, not have forced upon them. Use graphics to alert users to the fact that sound files are available, but understand that not everyone will want to listen, especially if their connection speed is a bit limp or if they need a specific audio player installed. Even if the download is free, the option to download anything from the internet, no matter how trustworthy you think the provider is, won't wash with more timid internet adventurers.

Any audio features that you add to a web site must come with an obvious off button. Users have this right and will be very annoyed if it is denied to them.

AND, ACTION!

Most of the rules about using audio files carry through for moving images, whether they are movie files or animation such as Flash. The major concern has to be the file size and the streaming quality for users who don't enjoy the same connection speed as you. A relatively recent and clever way round this problem is to offer the same files in hi-res and lo-res and through multiple viewers. If you've created a movie file it's easy enough to create these options. And, because you've made it so easy, you'll enjoy far more downloads as you'll be appealing to a much wider audience.

Adding value-added features can really work for your site, or it can work against it. Never is this truer than with a web site introduction. To learn more, check out IDEA 12, *Pretty flash, but do they make you run faster?*

Try another idea...

'Big nations are like chickens. They like to make big noises, but very often it is no more than squabbling.'
ALBERT SCHWEITZER

Defining idea...

'Music makes one feel so romantic – at least it always gets on one's nerves – which is the same thing nowadays.'
OSCAR WILDE

Defining idea...

How did
it go?

Q **The IT department are really keen on the idea but marketing argue that offering different viewers is going to confuse the users into downloading all four options instead of just one. Could this be the case?**

A *Not at all – your users are highly intelligent! Although it would be bold to say that absolutely no confusion will occur, the vast majority of internet users who recognise that clicking on a link will download an audio or video file will also understand that the options are just giving you the chance to appeal to as many users as possible.*

Q **Marketing don't want to use any audio or video files – is this a nail in our own coffin?**

A *Not at all. Only add features that add value to your offering. Keep noise to a minimum.*

52

Sticky buns

You want to attract users, keep them a while, then let them go so they can come back for more. A simple enough task. Here are some tips to help.

How to make a sticky bun: blend up-to-date cool text and images in an attractive and always-available web site. Pop on a cherry and visitors will come back again and again, spending money and just hanging out...

MI CASA SU CASA

Most internet users eventually work out that they can alter their homepage from whatever default is foisted upon them by either their operating system or by their ISP (Internet Service Provider). For many, this is their company web site (don't you just love the dedication?), a search engine or their own personal web site. But that still leaves a large number of users who might just be convinced to set your web site as their homepage. Never, ever force users to make the change, and certainly don't do it without their knowledge (tempting though it may be), but if somebody has registered with you (not just landed on your homepage), they shouldn't be offended if you ask if they would like your site as their homepage. A simple click on

Here's an idea for you... **Ask the marketing department to devise a competition that's in keeping with the products or services you are promoting. Set four stages to the competition; its main purpose should be to encourage existing visitors to visit more often (a separate competition should be devised to capture new visitors). The prize should be a product or service from your web site; don't choose the most expensive, choose the most popular.**

yes can reconfigure their options settings and there you are, pride of place, every time the user launches their web browser.

AH! HERE WE ARE

It is so easy to implement, yet so few sites do it. Let users know where they are on your site. A quick and easy way to help your visitor feel safe, secure and in control is by giving them a 'virtual hug'. Show them what they are doing in simple text:

Home>Products>Clamps>Executive>Offers

Your potential customer can immediately see from this that they have come into the products area of the store. He is looking through the selection of clamps for sale and is now within the offers area of the executive section. This knowledge takes next to no room up at the top of the page (below the navigation bar) but adds so much value to the site. It gives them yet another reason not to leave the site and to continue through to purchase. Put simply, it costs nothing to be courteous; but it could cost a lot not to be.

Defining idea... *'Why is it drug addicts and computer aficionados are both called users?'*
CLIFFORD STOLL

SO, WHAT'S NEW?

Giving users a reason to return does involve some work from you, but by constantly updating your products, information or news you'll be making your web site an exciting and innovative place to visit. Internet users feel that they are at the cutting edge of information retrieval. They are! You can find out pretty much anything you want to on the internet, pretty much as soon as it happens. To take part in this and become an information provider you must pander to users' need for quick, reliable, easy-to-access information and react accordingly. There really isn't much point updating your site only once a month. Someone else will beat you to it and in doing so will win the custom of your users.

> **To truly make your site sticky, make your users feel part of a community. To find out more, check out IDEA 46, *There's no place like home.***

Try another idea...

YOU'RE A WINNER

The ubiquitous competition is quickly becoming the favoured mechanism to keep user interest in a site. The prizes don't have to be huge (although it does help). If you are offering a prize for actually doing something, however little (registering, recommending a friend, etc.), then users feel they have a good chance of winning, and compared with most national or state lotteries, they do. Use a competition that unfolds over a number of weeks. That way, users must keep logging on to answer the next question, and only when the competition is complete (maybe after five visits) can they be entered to win the prize.

> *'I would rather try to persuade a man to go along, because once I have persuaded him he will stick. If I scare him, he will stay just as long as he is scared, and then he is gone.'*
> DWIGHT D. EISENHOWER

Defining idea...

> *'We are what we repeatedly do.'*
> ARISTOTLE

Defining idea...

How did
it go?

Q We monitored the number of users entering each week and there was a significant tailing off towards the end. Should we reduce the number of weeks that we run the competition?

A   *Hard to tell. First, the perceived value of the prize you are offering will dictate how patient users will be. Put simply, the more attractive the prize, the more you can ask of entrants. If the number of visitors entering in weeks two and three remained pretty constant and then dropped off before week four, then maybe three weeks is the most you can expect with that level of prize. Still, you have succeeded in bringing users back to you for little investment. You'll perfect it if you run it over time with different objectives and prizes, and meanwhile you'll be enjoying more and more users on your site.*

Q We host the web site off-premises. How can we guarantee it's always available?

A   *You can't – not 100 per cent. Ensure that your service provider issues you with an SLA – a service level agreement – that makes a promise to you about up time and shows how they will react if things go wrong.*

The end...

We hope that you've been inspired to revamp your web site. When visitors hit your site you should be able to knock them out with your inspirational use of clever design and inventive functionality. Let us know if that's the case. We'd like to be amazed and impressed too.

If there was an idea that you struggled to understand, tell us about that too. Tell us how you got on generally. What did it for you – what helped you to punch through the jargon and re-energise your web site? Maybe you've got some tips of your own that you want to share. If you liked this book you may find we have more brilliant ideas for other areas that could help change your life for the better.

You'll find the Infinite Ideas crew waiting for you online at www.infideas.com.

Or if you prefer to write, then send your letters to:
Web Sites that Work
The Infinite Ideas Company Ltd
Belsyre Court, 57 Woodstock Road, Oxford OX2 6JH, United Kingdom

We want to know what you think, because we're all working on making our lives better too. Give us your feedback and you could win a copy of another 52 *Brilliant Ideas* book of your choice. Or maybe get a crack at writing your own.

Good luck. Be brilliant.

Offer one

CASH IN YOUR IDEAS

We hope you enjoy this book. We hope it inspires, amuses, educates and entertains you. But we don't assume that you're a novice, or that this is the first book that you've bought on the subject. You've got ideas of your own. Maybe our author has missed an idea that you use successfully. If so, why not send it to info@infideas.com, and if we like it we'll post it on our bulletin board. Better still, if your idea makes it into print we'll send you £50 and you'll be fully credited so that everyone knows you've had another Brilliant Idea.

Offer two

HOW COULD YOU REFUSE?

Amazing discounts on bulk quantities of Infinite Ideas books are available to corporations, professional associations and other organizations.

For details call us on:
+44 (0)1865 292045
fax: +44 (0)1865 292001
or e-mail: info@infideas.com

Where it's at...